CHAMPIONS LEAGUE
FACT FILE

Clive Gifford

CARLTON KIDS

CONTENTS

THIS IS A CARLTON BOOK
Text, design and illustration
© Carlton Books Limited 2015

Published in 2015 by Carlton Books Limited
An imprint of the Carlton Publishing Group
20 Mortimer Street, London W1T 3JW

Design: RockJaw Creative
Editor: Simon Mugford
Cover design: RockJaw Creative

10 9 8 7 6 5 4 3 2 1

All rights reserved. This book is sold subject to the condition that it may not be reproduced, stored in a retrieval system or transmitted in any form or by any means, electronic, mechanical, photocopying, recording or otherwise, without the publisher's prior consent.

A catalogue record for this book is available from the British Library.

ISBN: 978-1-78312-131-1 (HB)
      978-1-78312-181-6 (PB)

Printed in Dubai

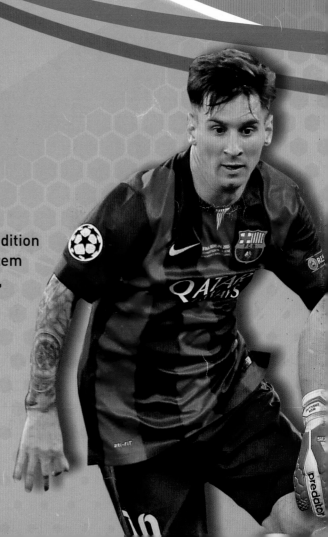

Note to the reader: The facts and records in this book are accurate up to the 2014-15 Champions League final.

A EUROPE-WIDE competition

The Champions League (and the European Cup that came before it) was designed as a competition for the leading football clubs of Europe. Over time, it has expanded so that clubs from more than 50 different member nations of UEFA – the body that runs European football – take part. Although it is only open to clubs from Europe, elite players from all over the world have taken part in this glittering competition.

Porto **2**

Liverpool **5**

Aston Villa **1**

This map shows the 22 teams that have won all 60 European Cup and Champions League tournaments, from 1955-56 (Real Madrid) to 2014-15 (Barcelona).

Chelsea **1**

Benfica **2**

Real Madrid **10**

Barcelona **5**

Real Madrid have taken part in more seasons of the European Cup and Champions League than any other club – a record 46 participations up to and including the 2015-16 season.

Marseille **1**

1 Celtic

3 Manchester United

2 Nottingham Forest

4 Ajax

1 Hamburg

1 Feyenoord

1 Borussia Dortmund

5 Bayern Munich

1 PSV Eindhoven

1 Red Star Belgrade

3 Internazionale

7 AC Milan

2 Juventus

1 Steaua Bucharest

Trondheim in Norway is home to the European mainland's most northerly Champions League club, Rosenborg BK. They have played more than 130 Champions League and European Cup matches.

Ukrainian club Dynamo Kyiv hold the record for most Champions League participations in a row (including the qualifying rounds) – 20 seasons from 1993-94 to 2012-13.

Barcelona celebrate Ivan Rakitić's early opening goal against Juventus in the 2015 final. Both clubs have reached the final eight times, with Barcelona winning the trophy on five occasions to Juve's two. It was a treble triumph for coach Luis Enrique in his first season in charge, as Barcelona also won La Liga and the Copa del Rey.

The 2015 final – Barça's treble

On 6 June 2015, in a packed Olympiastadion in Berlin, more than 70,000 fans witnessed a classic encounter between two heavyweights of European football, Juventus and Barcelona, as they contested the 2014-15 Champions League final. Captained by Andrés Iniesta, the Spanish side's devastating strike force of Luis Suárez, Neymar and Lionel Messi was in red-hot form throughout the tournament, scoring 27 goals between them. Two of these came in the final following Ivan Rakitić's opener for Barcelona in the fourth minute. Juventus equalised through Álvaro Morata and threatened at times but could not withstand the attacking power of their opponents, with goals from Suárez and Neymar sealing Barça's fifth Champions League / European Cup triumph.

Part 1:
Back in Time

After the success of smaller tournaments such as the Mitropa Cup, the Coupe des Nations and the Latin Cup, demand for a Europe-wide football competition grew in the 1950s. UEFA (the Union of European Football Associations) was founded on 15 June 1954 in Basel, Switzerland and within a year had given the go-ahead for a competition, the European Champions Club Cup, or European Cup for short. In the first season, a number of high-scoring games included AC Milan's 7-2 demolition of Rapid Vienna, who had previously beaten PSV Eindhoven 6-1. The final in Paris was also graced with goals, as Real Madrid defeated Stade de Reims 4-3 to became the first ever European Cup champions. Subsequent seasons saw several giants of European football emerge from Italy, Portugal, Germany and elsewhere to battle Real for supremacy. But the chance of an upset from new teams waiting in the wings was never far away.

Real Madrid celebrate winning the very first tournament in June 1956. The Spanish giants were 2-0 down to Stade de Reims within ten minutes, but two goals from Héctor Rial and strikes by Marcos Alonso Imaz and Alfredo di Stéfano saw them triumph 4-3.

STARTING success

On 4 September 1955, the European Cup kicked off with a wildly entertaining 3-3 draw between Sporting Clube de Portugal and Partizan Belgrade of Yugoslavia. Two of Partizan's goals were scored by Miloš Milutinović who, with eight goals, ended the competition as leading scorer.

L'Equipe picks

Sixteen teams took part in the first European Cup. They did not qualify, but instead were selected by the French football magazine *L'Equipe*! Some of the teams originally chosen did not take part: the English FA would not let Chelsea compete, while Holland Sport refused to enter and were replaced by another Dutch side, PSV Eindhoven.

Real Madrid dominate

Coming back from two goals down against Stade de Reims to win the 1956 final 4-3, Real Madrid became the first European champions. They would go on to win the first five European Cups in a row.

Viollet's purple patch

The 1956-57 European Cup saw England's first entrant, Manchester United, notch up a record 10-0 win against Anderlecht with Dennis Viollet scoring four goals. Viollet ended up as the leading scorer that season with nine goals.

U.R.B.S.F.A.

12 · 9 · 1956 · 19 heures 30
BRUXELLES
(Stade Emile Versé - Parc d'Anderlecht)

R.S.C. Anderlechtois
CHAMPION DE BELGIQUE
Manchester United
CHAMPION D'ANGLETERRE

POUR LA COUPE DES
CLUBS CHAMPIONS
EUROPEENS
Programme Officiel
édité par
André et Loiseau s.a.
IMPRIMERIE
EDITION
PUBLICITE
9, Boulevard de l'Abattoir, Bruxelles
PRIX: 5 FRANCS

Toss of a coin

As the number of clubs interested in competing increased, a preliminary round was added. In the 1957-58 preliminary round, the floodlights failed during a match between Gwardia Warszawa and East German club Wismut Karl Marx Stadt. With the score tied at 1-1, a coin toss was used to decide the winners, with the East German team progressing.

Goal glut

There were goals galore in the first European Cup competition – 127 in just 29 games! Only one match ended in a 0-0 draw – a first round, first leg game between Djurgårdens IF of Sweden and Polish club Gwardia Warszawa. Two games saw nine goals as Vörös Lobogó SE beat Anderlecht 6-3 and AC Milan beat Rapid Vienna 7-2.

The ultimate final

The most stunning game in the early European Cups was the 1959-60 final at Hampden Park, Glasgow. An absolute feast of football in which Real Madrid routed Eintracht Frankfurt 7-3, it remains the only final in which two players have scored hat-tricks (Ferenc Puskás, with four goals, and Alfredo di Stéfano).

Alfredo di Stéfano scores Real Madrid's opening goal of the 1960 final, shooting past Eintracht Frankfurt's keeper, Egon Loy.

THE 1960s

The 1960s saw the first champions from Italy, Portugal, Scotland and England. Teams from the Soviet Union, Norway, Iceland and Cyprus entered the competition for the first time and from the 1969-70 season, two substitutes were allowed per team.

A 50-year-long record

AC Milan became the first Italian side to win the European Cup, in 1962-63. They were propelled to the final by José Altafini's record 14 goals in the season. His tally stood as the most goals scored in the European Cup or Champions League until Cristiano Ronaldo scored 17 in the 2013-14 season – more than 50 years later.

Manager Sir Matt Busby and his Manchester United team pose with the trophy in 1968. England's first European champions defeated Benfica 4-1 after extra time.

Great Gento

Francisco Gento played in the Real Madrid sides which took part in eight European Cup finals between 1955-56 and 1970-71. The lightning-fast attacker scored 30 goals in the competition and won six European Cups, making him the tournament's most successful player.

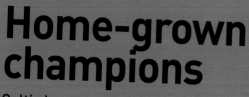

Home-grown champions

Celtic became the first champions from Britain when they beat final favourites Internazionale in Portugal in 1967. The entire Celtic team, nicknamed the 'Lions of Lisbon', were all born within 50km of Celtic Park, the club's home ground.

Old master

Real Madrid's sixth victory in 1966 featured the oldest winner of the competition – Ferenc Puskás, who was 39 years and 39 days old when Real beat Partizan Belgrade on 11 May 1966. In the first round of that year's competition, Puskás had scored five of Real's six goals when they lost away to Feyenoord 2-1 and won 5-0 at home.

FINALS (1955-56 TO 1969-70)

Year	Champions	Score	Runner-up
1955-56	Real Madrid	4-3	Stade de Reims
1956-57	Real Madrid	2-0	Fiorentina
1957-58	Real Madrid	3-2	AC Milan
1958-59	Real Madrid	2-0	Stade de Reims
1959-60	Real Madrid	7-3	Eintracht Frankfurt
1960-61	Benfica	3-2	Barcelona
1961-62	Benfica	5-3	Real Madrid
1962-63	AC Milan	2-1	Benfica
1963-64	Internazionale	3-1	Real Madrid
1964-65	Internazionale	1-0	Benfica
1965-66	Real Madrid	2-1	Partizan Belgrade
1966-67	Celtic	2-1	Internazionale
1967-68	Manchester Utd	4-1	Benfica
1968-69	AC Milan	4-1	Ajax
1969-70	Feyenoord	2-1	Celtic

THE 1970s

The 1970s began with a shock – Real Madrid failed to qualify for the 1970-71 European Cup. It would prove to be a decade of success for teams from three northern European footballing nations: the Netherlands, West Germany and England. Two teams would win the cup three times in a row, while English sides would appear in five finals during this period.

Dutch dominance

In 1970, Feyenoord became the first Dutch team to win the European Cup. This was followed by three titles in a row for their rivals Ajax. Under Rinus Michels and then Stefan Kovács, Ajax played a style of fluid 'total' football, with players such as Rudi Krol and Johan Cruyff switching positions at will.

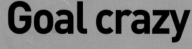

Ajax's Arie Haan celebrates scoring in the 1971 final.

Goal crazy

Ajax scored 26 goals in their first three games of the 1979-80 European Cup. After thrashing HJK Helsinki 8-1 both home and away, they mauled Omonoia of Cyprus 10-0 in the second round first leg. The Dutch side reached the semi-finals, but were defeated there by Nottingham Forest.

English doubles

Liverpool not only won the European Cup for the first time in 1977 but became the first British side to retain the trophy the following season. They were immediately followed by Brian Clough's Nottingham Forest who, with a team of unheralded players, won back-to-back European Cups at the end of the decade.

Trevor Francis heads the winning goal for Nottingham Forest against Malmö FF in the 1979 European Cup final.

FINALS (1970-71 TO 1979-80)

Year	Champions	Score	Runner-up
1970-71	Ajax	2-0	Panathinaikos
1971-72	Ajax	2-0	Internazionale
1972-73	Ajax	1-0	Juventus
1973-74	Bayern Munich	4-0	Atlético Madrid
1974-75	Bayern Munich	2-0	Leeds United
1975-76	Bayern Munich	1-0	Saint-Étienne
1976-77	Liverpool	3-1	Borussia Mönchengladbach
1977-78	Liverpool	1-0	Club Brugge
1978-79	Nottingham Forest	1-0	Malmö FF
1979-80	Nottingham Forest	1-0	Hamburg

Three in a row for Bayern

Bayern Munich won three European Cups in a row, defeating Atlético Madrid in 1974, Leeds United in 1975 and Saint-Étienne in 1976. Bayern remain the last team to win the competition in three consecutive seasons and their captain Franz Beckenbauer (left) is the only skipper to have lifted the trophy three times with the same club.

THE 1980s and early 1990s

The 1980s began with two multiple winners reaching the final, but later years saw several teams win the competition for the first time. These included Aston Villa and the first winners from eastern Europe in the form of Romanian club Steaua Bucharest.

Abandoned action

Only two of the four quarter-finals were completed in 1990-91. Red Star Belgrade were leading 2-1 against Dresden (having won the first game 3-0) when rioting caused the game to be abandoned. In the second leg of the Marseille v AC Milan encounter, floodlight failure caused a long delay and AC Milan refused to restart the game. Both Red Star and Marseille were awarded 3-0 wins and progressed.

Marseille striker Jean-Pierre Papin was the tournament's joint top scorer for three years in a row from 1989-90.

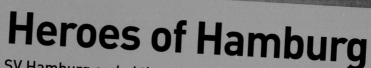

Hamburg's Felix Magath (right) scores the winner for SV Hamburg in the 1983 final.

Heroes of Hamburg

SV Hamburg ended the English dominance at the start of the decade with their first European Cup triumph in 1983. The German side were coached by Austrian Ernst Happel, who became the first coach to win the European Cup with two different teams – his first victory had come 13 years earlier with Feyenoord.

AC Milan legend Ruud Gullit celebrates one of his two goals in a 4-0 thrashing of Steaua Bucharest in the 1989 final.

FINALS (1980-81 TO 1991-92)

Year	Champions	Score	Runner-up	
1980-81	Liverpool	1-0	Real Madrid	
1981-82	Aston Villa	1-0	Bayern Munich	
1982-83	SV Hamburg	1-0	Juventus	
1983-84	Liverpool	1-1*	Roma	(*4-2 pens)
1984-85	Juventus	1-0	Liverpool	
1985-86	Steaua Bucharest	0-0*	Barcelona	(*2-0 pens)
1986-87	Porto	2-1	Bayern Munich	
1987-88	PSV Eindhoven	0-0*	Benfica	(*6-5 pens)
1988-89	AC Milan	4-0	Steaua Bucharest	
1989-90	AC Milan	1-0	Benfica	
1990-91	Red Star Belgrade	0-0*	Marseille	(*5-3 pens)
1991-92	Barcelona	1-0	Sampdoria	

Old goal

During a West v East German European Cup match in 1988, SV Werder Bremen's Manfred Burgsmüller became the oldest ever player to score in the competition, when he struck against SC Dynamo Berlin at the age of 38 years, 293 days. Burgsmüller retired at 41 but went on to become an American football player until the age of 52!

Groups galore

There were no quarter-finals or semi-finals in the 1991-92 season. Instead, the eight remaining teams were drawn into two groups and played their opponents both home and away. The two group winners, Barcelona and Sampdoria, contested the final at Wembley, which was won for the Spanish side with an extra-time goal by Ronald Koeman.

Part 2:
The Competition

In 1992, the European Cup had a major makeover and became the Champions League. Since then, the competition has expanded to include eight groups of four teams. Each team aims to get through their group and into the knockout stages. These consist of the two-leg Round of 16, quarter-finals and semi-finals, and culminate in a single-game final. For any club that progresses, the rewards are immense. In 2014-15, clubs were given a million Euros for every win in the group stage, 3.9 million Euros for reaching the quarter-finals and 4.9 million Euros at the semi-final stage. The champions received all those payments, plus a further 10.5 million Euros.

It's not just about money though. At stake is the most highly prized trophy in European club football.

Iker Casillas lifts the trophy after Real Madrid's record tenth title in 2014. After Real were allowed to keep the original European Cup (after their sixth win, in 1966) a new trophy made of silver was commissioned. It stands 73.5cm high, weighs 7.5kg and is nicknamed 'Big Ears' for its large curved handles. Any team that wins the trophy three times in a row (such as Bayern Munich and Ajax) or five times in total (such as AC Milan) is allowed to keep it and a new trophy is produced. The last time this happened was in 2015, following Barcelona's fifth title.

A CHAMPIONS League place

There are 32 places up for grabs in each Champions League competition. Twenty-two are filled automatically according to a complex seeding system called the UEFA Coefficient. This ranks the different countries' leagues and clubs according to performance, and grants the most powerful and successful footballing nations more places in the competition.

Automatic entry

The national league champions of the top 13 countries ranked according to the UEFA Coefficient gain automatic entry to the group stages. So do the runners-up from each of the top six countries and the third-placed teams from the top three leagues: currently Germany, England and Spain. That leaves ten group-stage places to be filled through a series of qualifying matches.

Bayer Leverkusen's Sebastian Boenisch (right) fends off Andreas Cornelius of FC Copenhagen in a 2014–15 play-off game. The German giants won 7-2 over two legs.

Dutch legend Johan Cruyff draws the teams for the 2013-14 group stage.

Five alive

In 2005-06, an unprecedented five clubs from England entered the Champions League competition. This was because UEFA granted an extra place to Liverpool, who had finished outside the top four in the English Premier League, but had won the Champions League the previous year. Since then, the champions gain an automatic place in the competition.

Big and small

In the 2014-15 Champions League, 77 teams from 53 nations took part in qualifying. These included Lincoln Red Imps, Gibraltar's first-ever side in the competition, who took part in the first round. By contrast, the fourth round (or play-off stage) of qualification that season included major teams such as Arsenal and Napoli, as well as former champions Porto, Bayer Leverkusen and Steaua Bucharest.

Crash! Bangor walloped

Welsh club Bangor City suffered the biggest thrashing in a Champions League qualifier, beaten 10-0 by Finland's HJK Helsinki in the second leg of the second qualifying round in 2011-12. They lost 13-0 on aggregate, another Champions League record.

Celtic shocker

Qualifying games can throw up shock results. In the second round of qualifying for the 2005-06 Champions League, former European Cup winners Celtic were thrashed 5-0 by Artmedia Bratislava. The Slovakian club (with a budget of just £1 million a year) became one of the first teams to make it through all the qualifying rounds to reach a Champions League group stage.

Artmedia Bratislava celebrate their shock 5-0 win over Celtic.

MOST PARTICIPATIONS (EUROPEAN CUP AND CHAMPIONS LEAGUE, 1955-56 TO 2015-16)

46 Real Madrid	32 Bayern Munich	30 Juventus
35 Benfica		30 Porto
32 Ajax	32 Dynamo Kyiv	30 Glasgow Rangers
32 Anderlecht	30 Celtic	

IN THE group

From September to December every year, the top 32 sides in Europe battle it out in the group stages of the Champions League. Each team is placed in a four-team group (labelled A to H) and plays six games: three home and three away. The top two teams from each group qualify for the knockout stages.

Cruising through

Group games are usually very competitive, so it is quite an achievement to win all six. Five teams have managed to do so, but only Real Madrid have achieved it twice – in 2011-12 and 2014-15.

New recruits

Two teams made their Champions League debuts in the 2014-15 group stage: Swedish club Malmö FF and Ludogorets Razgrad from Bulgaria. Ludogorets were only formed in 2001 and made their first appearance in the Bulgarian top division in 2011-12.

Thomas Müller, Arjen Robben (twice) and Mario Götze all scored in Bayern's 7-1 thrashing of Roma in 2014 – the club's biggest ever away win in Europe.

Goal feast

The third round of group matches in the 2014-15 season set a record for the number of goals scored in eight Champions League games. A net-busting 40 were scored, including seven by both Bayern Munich (v Roma) and Shakhtar Donetsk (v BATE Borisov), and six by Chelsea (v NK Maribor).

Francesco Totti equalizes for Roma against Manchester City in September 2014.

Old pro

Italian attacker Francesco Totti first scored in European competition in 1997. Astonishingly, he was still at it in the 2014-15 season, netting for Roma against Manchester City and CSKA Moscow in Group E, and becoming the oldest goalscorer of the Champions League era, at 38 years and 59 days.

Goal gluts, goal droughts

Manchester United (1998-99), Barcelona (2011-12) and Real Madrid (2013-14) have all scored 20 goals in their group, while Liverpool scored eight goals in a group game against Beşiktaş in 2007–08. In contrast, Villareal qualified as group winners in 2005-06, scoring just three goals but notching up two wins.

EARLY exits

Not every team can make it out of their group. Sometimes the big, favoured sides flounder while less-fancied teams manage to qualify ahead of them. The third-placed teams in each group have the consolation of entering the UEFA Europa League competition at the Round of 32 stage.

Champions upset

During the Champions League era, all except one of the champions have progressed through the following year's group stages. The exception is Chelsea, who in 2012-13 were knocked out of their group despite scoring more goals (16) than any of the other group-stage sides and finishing on ten points.

Chelsea's Oscar shoots past Juventus legend Andrea Pirlo in 2012-13. The Brazilian scored five goals in the group stage, but his team still crashed out.

Out for the count

The early rounds of the old European Cup were two-legged ties against a single opponent. In 1965-66, Luxembourg side Stade Dudelange were beaten 8-0 at home by Benfica, before being mauled 10-0 away and exiting the European Cup with the highest-ever aggregate defeat – 18-0.

Consolation prize

As third-place finishers in their 2012-13 Champions League group, Chelsea took part in the Europa League. They became the first Champions League dropouts to win the trophy, beating Benfica in the final 2-1, thanks to a powerful header from Branislav Ivanović in the last minute of added time.

Marseille are devastated as Borussia Dortmund score a late winner in a 2013-14 Group F game.

Scoreless sides

Sixteen teams have suffered six defeats out of six in the group stage, the latest being Marseille in the 2013-14 season. Only two teams have failed to score a single goal: Maccabi Haifa in 2009-10 and Deportivo de La Coruña in 2004-05. La Coruña did at least register two points from two 0-0 draws.

European legends Liverpool crashed out of the 2014-15 group stage after a 1-1 draw with FC Basel.

Cruel departure

Two teams have racked up a healthy group-stage tally of 12 points, yet still failed to qualify for the knockout stages: Paris Saint-Germain in 1997-98 and Napoli in 2013-14. Napoli finished level on points with Arsenal and Borussia Dortmund, but were eliminated on goal difference.

KNOCKOUT stages

The top two teams from each group enter the knockout stages of the Champions League, which starts with the Round of 16 and culminates in the final. Apart from the final, these rounds are played over two games, one home and one away.

Toss of a coin

In the early years of the European Cup, a coin toss was used to decide the result of a drawn knockout match. The last teams to benefit from a toss were Galatasaray and Celtic, both in the second round of the 1969-70 European Cup. Celtic reached the final that season.

Apoel Nicosia celebrate their 4-3 penalty shootout win over Lyon in 2011-12. They went on to lose 8-2 over two legs to Real Madrid in the quarter-finals.

Away goals

The first European Cup game decided on away goals was played on 1 October 1967, between Valur of Iceland and Jeunesse Esch of Luxembourg. Valur went through after a 3-3 away draw (the first leg ended 1-1), but lost the next round against Vasas SC of Hungary 11-1 on aggregate!

Deportivo de La Coruña (below) dump out reigning champions AC Milan in 2003-04.

Courageous comeback

Goals from Kaká, Andrea Pirlo and Andriy Shevchenko had put AC Milan 4-1 up after the first leg of their 2003-04 quarter-final against Deportivo de La Coruña. But the Spanish side had other ideas and, roared on by 29,000 fans at their Riazor Stadium, won the second leg 4-0 to reach the semis.

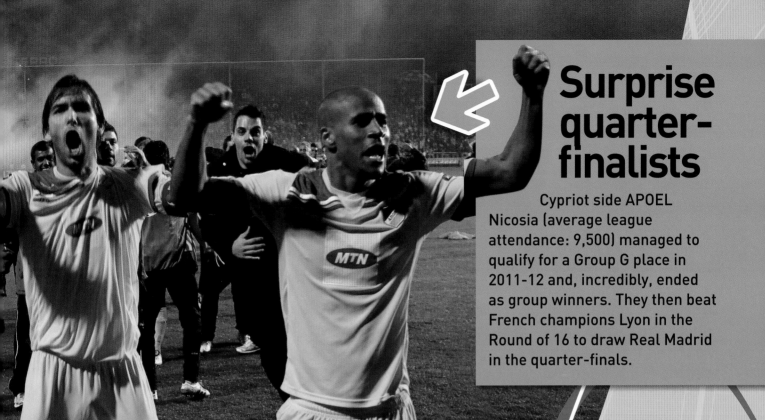

Surprise quarter-finalists

Cypriot side APOEL Nicosia (average league attendance: 9,500) managed to qualify for a Group G place in 2011-12 and, incredibly, ended as group winners. They then beat French champions Lyon in the Round of 16 to draw Real Madrid in the quarter-finals.

Both Lukas Podolski and Miroslav Klose scored in Bayern's 7-1 rout of Sporting.

Cruising through

The last team to go through both the group stage and the knockout rounds of the Champions League unbeaten were Manchester United in the 2007-08 season. They produced nine wins and four draws on their way to winning the competition.

Bayern blitz

Bayern Munich racked up the biggest aggregate score in a Champions League knockout round when they thrashed Sporting Clube de Portugal 5-0 and 7-1 in the 2008-09 Round of 16. Bayern also hold the record for the biggest margin of victory in one knockout leg: 7-0 wins over FC Basel in 2011-12 and Shakhtar Donetsk in 2014-15.

SUPER semi-finals

Tensions rise when the tournament reaches the semi-final stage. Real Madrid, with 26 semi-final appearances since 1955-56, and Bayern Munich, with 17, have reached this stage the most. Thirty-eight teams have reached the semis just once, including Dundee United (1984) and Young Boys (1959). Only one team has reached the semi-finals just once and gone on to win the title (Aston Villa in 1982).

Surprising semi

Real Madrid were favourites going into their 2012-13 semi-final clash with Borussia Dortmund. In the first leg, Cristiano Ronaldo scored his 50th Champions League goal, but Dortmund's Polish striker Robert Lewandowski became the highest scorer in a Champions League semi, with four glorious goals in a 4-1 victory.

Strange San Siro semi

AC Milan and Internazionale faced each other in the 2002-03 semi-final with both legs played at the San Siro – the ground shared by the teams. Two draws, 0-0 and 1-1, followed but because AC Milan were considered the 'away' team in the second leg, they went through on away goals. They went on to win the final against another Italian team, Juventus.

Robert Lewandowski scores the first of four goals for Borussia Dortmund against Real Madrid in the 2012-13 semi-final.

Barcelona's hopes of seven semis in a row were dashed by a 2-1 defeat to Atlético Madrid (above) in 2014.

Six in a row

The most consecutive semi-finals reached by one team is six, by Barcelona between 2008 and 2013. They nearly made it seven, but were defeated by Atlético Madrid at the 2013-14 quarter-final stage.

Three out of four

Three of the semi-finalists have come from the same country on three occasions during the Champions League era: Spain (1999-2000), Italy (2002-03) and England (2006-07).

Chelsea's Fernando Torres celebrates his injury-time winner against Barcelona in 2011-12.

Departing champions

Seven defending champions have been knocked out at the semi-final stage in the Champions League era – more than in any other round. This has happened three times to Real Madrid (2000-01, 2002-03, 2014-15) and twice to Barcelona, who were beaten 3-2 by Internazionale in 2009-10 and Chelsea in 2011-12.

FIT FOR a final

So far, 15 nations from Belgium to Russia, Scotland to Turkey have hosted the European Cup or Champions League final. Italy and England are the hosts with the most – a record eight times each. Germany equalled their record when the Olympic Stadium in Berlin was chosen to hold the 2014-15 final.

Playing at home

The venue for the final is chosen well in advance and, occasionally, a club plays a final in their own country. It doesn't always prove an advantage. While Juventus won the 1996 final in Rome, and Borussia Dortmund the 1997 final in Munich, Bayern Munich lost the 2012 final in their home stadium, the Allianz Arena.

Wembley way

More finals have been held at London's Wembley Stadium than at any other venue: seven in total, starting with the 1963 European Cup final between AC Milan and Benfica. In the 2000s, the original Wembley was demolished for a new 90,000-capacity stadium, complete with a 134-metre-high arch. The new stadium has twice hosted finals, in 2011 and 2013 (below).

Grass at last

In 2006, Russia's Luzhniki Stadium became the first stadium with an artificial pitch to host a Champions League group match. But for the Manchester United v Chelsea final in 2007-08, UEFA insisted that a temporary grass pitch be installed.

Not once, but twice

The Heysel Stadium in Brussels held two European Cup final games in three days! The first game in May 1974 was a 1-1 draw between Bayern Munich and Atlético Madrid. Instead of a penalty shootout, a replay was staged, which saw Bayern triumph 4-0 courtesy of two goals each from Uli Hoeness and Gerd Müller.

Berlin's Olympiastadion (above) hosted the 2006 FIFA World Cup final and its first Champions League final in 2015.

BIGGEST FINAL ATTENDANCES
(1955-56 TO 2014-15)

127,621	Hampden Park, Glasgow, 1960
124,000	Bernabéu, Madrid, 1957
97,000	Camp Nou, Barcelona, 1989
92,500	Wembley Stadium, London, 1978
92,225	Wembley Stadium, London, 1968
90,245	Camp Nou, Barcelona, 1999
89,484	Red Star Stadium, Belgrade, 1973
89,000	San Siro, Milan, 1965

Smallest crowd

The Wankdorf Stadium in Bern, Switzerland hosted the final with the smallest number of fans present. Just 26,732 watched Benfica beat Barcelona 3-2 in 1961.

FANTASTIC finals

Football fans, not just in Europe but all over the globe, watch the Champions League final live on TV or follow the progress of teams via the Internet. The 2012-13 final, for example, drew a TV audience of over 360 million. Final matches are always tense and have seen all kinds of drama, action and controversy.

Two teams, one nation

Five Champions League-era finals have been contested by teams from the same country:

2000 Spain:
Real Madrid v Valencia, 3-0
2003 Italy:
AC Milan v Juventus, 0-0 (3-2 penalties)
2008 England:
Manchester United v Chelsea, 1-1 (6-5 penalties)
2013 Germany:
Bayern Munich v Borussia Dortmund, 2-1
2014 Spain:
Real Madrid v Atlético Madrid, 4-1

Bayern blitz

In the 2012 final against Chelsea, Bayern Munich had a staggering 35 shots on goal in the 90 minutes of regular time – more than any other team had attempted in one game during the 2011-12 tournament.

FINALS (1992-93 TO 2014-2015)

Year	Champions	Score	Runner-up
1992-93	Marseille	1-0	AC Milan
1993-94	AC Milan	4-0	Barcelona
1994-95	Ajax	1-0	AC Milan
1995-96	Juventus	1-1*	Ajax (4-2 pens)
1996-97	Borussia Dortmund	3-1	Juventus
1997-98	Real Madrid	1-0	Juventus
1998-99	Manchester United	2-1	Bayern Munich
1999-00	Real Madrid	3-0	Valencia
2000-01	Bayern Munich	1-1*	Valencia (5-4 pens)
2001-02	Real Madrid	2-1	Bayer Leverkusen
2002-03	AC Milan	0-0*	Juventus (3-2 pens)
2003-04	Porto	3-0	Monaco
2004-05	Liverpool	3-3*	AC Milan (3-2 pens)
2005-06	Barcelona	2-1	Arsenal
2006-07	AC Milan	2-1	Liverpool
2007-08	Manchester United	1-1*	Chelsea (6-5 pens)
2008-09	Barcelona	2-0	Manchester United
2009-10	Internazionale	2-0	Bayern Munich
2010-11	Barcelona	3-1	Manchester United
2011-12	Chelsea	1-1*	Bayern Munich (4-3)
2012-13	Bayern Munich	2-1	Borussia Dortmund
2013-14	Real Madrid	4-1	Atlético Madrid
2014-15	Barcelona	3-1	Juventus

From the jaws of defeat

As the half-time whistle blew in the 2004-05 final, Liverpool looked down and out, trailing AC Milan 3-0. But in a scintillating second-half spell they scored three times, while at the other end of the pitch Jerzy Dudek made a string of stunning saves as the game ended 3-3. Liverpool won the trophy in a nervy penalty shootout.

Liverpool captain Steven Gerrard lifts the trophy in 2005 after a dramatic 3-2 penalty shootout win over AC Milan.

Repeat runners-up

Juventus have reached eight finals, but only won twice (1984-85, 1995-96). Their record sixth runners-up appearance came in 2014-15, with a 3-1 defeat to Barcelona. Bayern Munich and Benfica are close behind, each losing five finals.

Juve's Andrea Pirlo is dejected after the 2015 final defeat to Barcelona.

CHAMPIONS part 1

Real Madrid were the first champions of Europe and remain the most successful side in the history of the competition. Their long-awaited tenth trophy (La Décima) was secured in the 2013-14 final, when they defeated city-rivals Atlético Madrid 4-1 with three extra-time goals coming from Gareth Bale, Marcelo and Cristiano Ronaldo.

Captain Frank Lampard (below) holds the trophy in 2012 after Chelsea became the fifth English side to win the competition.

Champion countries

The most successful country is Spain with 15 titles spread between just two clubs, Barcelona and Real Madrid. Italian clubs are not far behind, with 12 triumphs from 27 appearances in the final – the most – while England have provided the greatest number of different winners – five.

Champions' curse

The European Cup was defended 13 times, but no champions in the Champions League era have managed to retain their crown. Four defending champions have reached the final in the following year but lost: AC Milan (1994-95), Ajax (1995-96), Juventus (1996-97) and Manchester United (2008-09).

Sergio Ramos wheels away in delight after scoring in the 2014 final for Real Madrid against Atlético Madrid.

Triple Dutch

Dutch midfielder Clarence Seedorf is the only player to have won the Champions League with three different clubs: Ajax in 1995, Real Madrid in 1998 and AC Milan in both 2003 and 2007.

Dutch teammates Clarence Seedorf and Edgar Davids tangle during the 1998 final.

Falling short

Three teams have reached the final twice but never won it: Stade de Reims (1956, 1959), Valencia (2000, 2001) and Atlético Madrid (1974, 2014). Juventus and Benfica have won the competition twice, but have been runners-up six and five times respectively.

Hat-trick heroes

The last player to score a hat-trick in the final was AC Milan's Pierino Prati in 1969. The only player to have scored a hat-trick in two finals was Real Madrid's Ferenc Puskás, who bagged four goals in the 1960 final. He scored a hat-trick against Benfica in the 1962 final, yet finished on the losing side.

CHAMPIONS
part 2

The Bayern team give their fans in Munich a view of the three trophies won in a glorious 2012-13 season.

Most finals

Francisco Gento and Paolo Maldini have appeared in more European Cup or Champions League finals (eight) than any other players. Maldini scored the quickest goal in a final, when he volleyed in a crossed free kick after just 51 seconds in 2005.

Final flourish

Four teams have reached the final just once and won the competition: Feyenoord (1970), Aston Villa (1982), PSV Eindhoven (1988) and Red Star Belgrade (1991). Aston Villa also hold the record for the champions with the worst domestic-league finish in the same year. Villa finished 11th in the English First Division.

Young guns

Two players from Ajax's 1994-95 Champions League-winning side are the competition's youngest-ever winners. Both Nwankwo Kanu and Patrick Kluivert were 18 years old at the time of the final.

Patrick Kluivert celebrates with the trophy in 1995.

A treble of trophies

Five teams in the Champions League era have won the treble (the Champions League, their national league and their national cup competition all in the same season): Barcelona (twice, most recently in 2014-15), Manchester United, Internazionale and Bayern Munich.

MOST TITLES (EUROPEAN CUP AND CHAMPIONS LEAGUE)

10 **Real Madrid** 1956, 1957, 1958, 1959, 1960, 1966, 1998, 2000, 2002, 2014

7 **AC Milan** 1963, 1969, 1989, 1990, 1994, 2003, 2007

5 **Barcelona** 1992, 2006, 2009, 2011, 2015

5 **Bayern Munich** 1974, 1975, 1976, 2001, 2013

5 **Liverpool** 1977, 1978, 1981, 1984, 2005

4 **Ajax** 1971, 1972, 1973, 1995

3 **Internazionale** 1964, 1965, 2010

3 **Manchester Utd** 1968, 1999, 2008

Player turned manager

Six players have won as a player and then later as a coach. The first was Real Madrid's Miguel Muñoz, followed by Giovanni Trapattoni, Johan Cruyff, Carlo Ancelotti, Frank Rijkaard and Josep 'Pep' Guardiola (right).

CHAMPIONS League coaches

Behind every Champions League-winning side lies a skilful and shrewd manager or coach. He picks the players and selects the tactics required to outwit opponents. In the first 60 European Cup and Champions League competitions, 39 coaches have led teams to glory.

Paisley's hat-trick

Only two coaches so far have won the European Cup or Champions League three times. The first was Liverpool's Bob Paisley, who led the Reds to three successes in five years (1977, 1978 and 1981).

Carlo Ancelotti lifts the trophy in 2014 for Real Madrid, the sixth club he has coached in the Champions League.

Young Bob

The youngest coach to reach the final of the Champions League or European Cup was Bob Houghton, who coached Malmö FF in 1978-79, aged just 31 years, 229 days. The youngest coach to win the trophy was José Villalonga in 1955-56. He was 36 years, 192 days old at the time of the final.

Three clubs, three finals

Austrian manager Ernst Happel is the only coach to take three different teams to a European Cup or Champions League final. He won with Dutch side Feyenoord in 1970, Hamburg in 1983 and claimed the runners-up spot with Club Brugge in 1978.

Jose Mourinho (far left) and Jupp Heynckes stand on the touchline during their 2012 semi-final.

Doubling up

Seventeen coaches have won the trophy twice, but only three besides Carlo Ancelotti and Ernst Happel have won it with different clubs: Ottmar Hitzfeld (Bayern Munich, 1991; Borussia Dortmund, 1997), José Mourinho (Porto, 2004; Internazionale, 2010) and Jupp Heynckes (Real Madrid, 1998; Bayern Munich, 2013).

Old masters

At the age of 71 years, 231 days, former Belgian goalkeeper Raymond Goethals coached Marseille to France's first Champions League trophy in 1993, only for the club to be stripped of the title following a bribery scandal. The next-oldest winning coach was Sir Alex Ferguson, who was 66 when Manchester United won in 2008.

Champion Carlo

Carlo Ancelotti became the first coach to win three Champions League-era crowns when he guided Real Madrid to their tenth title in 2014. The Italian's first two wins were both with AC Milan, having taken them to three finals (2003, 2005, 2007). Ancelotti also won the competition twice as an AC Milan player.

Part 3:
Facts, Feats and Records

The Champions League and European Cup have thrown up some amazing feats, from big thrashings to miserly defences keeping a record number of clean sheets in a row. Team achievements mix with those of soccer superstars, such as the incredible goal records of Lionel Messi and Cristiano Ronaldo or Ryan Giggs' enduring prowess – he is the only player to have scored in Champions League games in 16 different seasons. Many records have been broken in recent years, such as Barcelona's Xavi playing in 157 Champions League games including qualifying – more than any other footballer.

Shakhtar Donetsk's Brazilian striker Luiz Adriano roars with delight after scoring in his side's 7-0 thrashing of BATE Borisov in the 2014-15 group stage. Adriano became only the second player (after Lionel Messi in 2012) to strike five times in a match in the Champions League era, and the first to score five away from home.

WINNING streaks

Successful Champions League sides win and keep on winning to get out of their group and advance through the knockout stages of the competition. Some teams have gone on extraordinary winning and goalscoring streaks.

Mario Götze (left) celebrates scoring Bayern's second goal against CSKA Moscow, on the way to a record tenth win in a row.

BAYERN'S TEN WINS IN A ROW
(APRIL-NOVEMBER 2013)

Juventus (home) 2-0
Juventus (away) 2-0
Barcelona (home) 4-0
Barcelona (away) 3-0
Borussia Dortmund (neutral) 2-1
CSKA Moscow (home) 3-0
Manchester City (away) 3-1
Viktoria Plzeň (home) 5-0
Viktoria Plzeň (away) 1-0
CSKA Moscow (away) 3-1

Perfect 10s

In November 2013, Bayern Munich beat CSKA Moscow 3-1 to secure a record tenth Champions League win in a row, scoring 28 goals and letting in just three. Real Madrid matched the winning run in February 2015 with a 2-0 victory at FC Schalke 04. They scored 27 goals and conceded three during their victory streak.

Borussia and Barça

The third- and fourth-longest winning streaks belong to Barcelona, with nine wins in a row between 2002 and 2003, and Borussia Dortmund, with eight between 1996 and 1997.

Scoring streak

Real Madrid started an unusual scoring streak in the 2010–11 season when Marcelo's 64th-minute goal gave them a 1-1 draw with Barcelona. The Spanish side then scored at least one goal in every Champions League game they played until they lost their quarter-final second leg 2-0 to Borussia Dortmund in April 2014 – a remarkable scoring run of 34 games in a row.

Unbeaten run

Staying unbeaten can be crucial to a club's Champion League chances. In 1997–98, Bayern Munich drew 0-0 with Borussia Dortmund. They then went on an astonishing run at the Olympic Stadium of 31 home games without defeat. The streak finally ended with a 3-2 defeat to Spain's Deportivo de La Coruña in 2002.

France's Karim Benzema (left) scored twice in Real Madrid's 6-1 rout of Galatasaray in September 2013, in the middle of Real's scoring streak.

SUPER subs

A head coach has a bench full of options and can pick up to three substitutes to bring on to change the formation, tactics and, sometimes, the fortunes of their team. A shaky defence might need shoring up, or fresh legs may be brought on to replace tired ones. On other occasions, the coach brings on an attacker in the hunt for a vital goal. Substitutes have made big impacts in some Champions League games.

Young gun

Young Ghanaian striker Peter Ofori-Quaye made his Champions League debut for Olympiacos as a substitute against Rosenborg in October 1997. He was on the pitch for just nine minutes before he swivelled and shot smartly past Jørn Jamtfall to become, at 17 years, 195 days, the Champions League's youngest-ever goalscorer.

Double sub success

Manchester United were trailing 1-0 to Bayern Munich in the 1999 Champions League final, when both of Sir Alex Ferguson's second-half substitutes – Teddy Sheringham and Ole Gunnar Solskjaer – scored in injury time to give the English side their first European triumph of the Champions League era.

Final flourish

Patrick Kluivert was just 18 years old when he came off the bench in the 70th minute for Ajax in the 1995 Champions League final against Italian giants AC Milan. Fifteen minutes later, he lost two markers in the penalty area to rifle home the game's only goal and give the Dutch side a memorable victory.

Ole Gunnar Solskjaer (left) celebrates as he scores the winner in the 1999 Champions League final.

Speedy super sub

In the 1997 Champions League final, Borussia Dortmund's Lars Ricken came on in the 71st minute and scored after being on the field for a mere 16 seconds. His strike, a well-judged chip over Juventus goalkeeper Angelo Peruzzi, was his first touch of the ball!

Saving his side

Aston Villa needed the shot-stopping prowess of their young substitute goalkeeper Nigel Spink to win the 1982 European Cup final against mighty Bayern Munich. After a shoulder injury to keeper Jimmy Rimmer, Spink came on in the ninth minute and kept a clean sheet in what was only his second senior game for Aston Villa.

Lars Ricken (above) holds the trophy in 1997 – he scored six Champions League goals in total.

As well as making vital assists, Henrik Larsson scored 11 Champions League goals in his career.

Irresistible assists

It's not always goalscorers that grab the glory. Henrik Larsson came on in the 61st minute for Barcelona, who were trailing Arsenal 1-0, in the 2006 Champions League final. Larsson produced two crucial assists for both Samuel Eto'o and Juliano Belletti to score, crowning Barcelona champions of Europe.

RECORD goalscorers

The European Cup's first ever goal came after just 14 minutes, struck by João Baptista Martins for Sporting Clube de Portugal in what turned into a 3-3 thriller against Partizan Belgrade in 1955. Since then thousands of shots, headers and deflections have been scored, creating drama and plenty of records.

Goals galore

Over 90 hat-tricks have been scored in Champions League history. The fastest took Bafétimbi Gomis just eight minutes as Lyon thrashed Dinamo Zagreb 7-1 in December 2011. Gomis scored a fourth as well, making him one of just 11 players to strike four or more goals in a game during the Champions League era.

Rivals Ronaldo (left) and Messi went head to head in the 2011 semi-final. Messi scored twice to put Barcelona through to the final.

FASTEST CHAMPIONS LEAGUE GOALS

Time	Player	For	Year
10.12 secs	Roy Makaay	Bayern Munich v Real Madrid	2007
10.96 secs	Jonas	Valencia v Bayer Leverkusen	2011
20.07 secs	Gilberto Silva	Arsenal v PSV Eindhoven	2002
20.12 secs	Alessandro del Piero	Juventus v Manchester United	1997
21.06 secs	Clarence Seedorf	AC Milan v FC Schalke 04	2005

Goal per game

Of all the Champions League hotshots, Gerd Müller remains the most lethal. He played 35 games in the European Cup and scored 35 times, the best ratio of any player with more than 20 goals. By comparison, Lionel Messi averages 0.78 goals per Champions League game, and Ronaldo 0.66.

Raúl's record

Raúl Gonzales was the first player to score over 70 goals in the Champions League. His 71st goal came in April 2011 for FC Schalke 04. Raúl also became the youngest player to score a Champions League hat-trick in 1995, aged 18 years and 114 days.

Raúl's 71st goal helped Schalke knock the champions, Internazionale, out of the 2010–11 Champions League at the quarter-final stage.

Goal race

Champions League rivals Cristiano Ronaldo and Lionel Messi have both overtaken Raúl's goalscoring record. Ronaldo has scored 78 goals for Real Madrid and Manchester United (including qualifying), and struck nine times in the 2013–14 group stage alone. Messi is just behind on 77, all for Barcelona, and was the Champions League top scorer for four seasons in a row (2008–09 to 2011–12).

Speedy strikes

Roy Makaay's sudden strike after just 10.12 seconds for Bayern Munich in 2007 (below) is the competition's fastest-ever goal. It is even more extraordinary considering that Bayern's opponents, Real Madrid, kicked off. The fastest own goal came in October 2013, scored in the second minute of the game by Real Sociedad's midfielder Iñigo Martínez in a 1-0 defeat to Manchester United.

...Com

The Champions League's 6,000th goal

On 5 March 2013 Borussia Dortmund were playing Shakhtar Donetsk in the second leg of their Champions League Round of 16 encounter. The German side had come from behind twice to earn a 2-2 away draw in Ukraine and were now playing Shakhtar in front of a home crowd of 65,413. Dortmund's central defender Felipe Santana headed in a Mario Götze corner to score in the 31st minute. Six minutes later, Götze swept in a low cross from Robert Lewandowski to score Dortmund's second and the competition's 6,000th goal since the Champions League kicked off in 1992.

GOAL MILESTONES

Goal	Scorer	For	Year
1st	Daniel Amokachi	Club Brugge	1992
1,000th	Dmitri Khokhlov	PSV Eindhoven	1998
2,000th	Erwin Sánchez	Boavista	2001
3,000th	David Trezeguet	Juventus	2003
4,000th	Peter Crouch	Liverpool	2007
5,000th	Luisão	Benfica	2010

Mario Götze gets ready to celebrate after scoring his landmark goal. It was a historic night for Borussia Dortmund, who reached the quarter-finals of the Champions League for the first time since 1998.

DEFENSIVE might

Goals and goalscorers may grab the glory, but teams also need a solid defence to prosper in the Champions League. A 0-0 draw might not be glamorous (AC Milan have a record 21 of them) but they can be crucial to getting a side out of a group or winning a two-legged knockout tie.

Unbeaten run

Manchester United's defensive strength was proved during a record 25-game unbeaten run between September 2007 and May 2009. The next-best run in the European Cup or Champions League was 20 games by Dutch side Ajax.

Monaco's Danijel Subasić claims the ball in a 2-0 win over Zenit St Petersburg in December 2014.

Hard to beat

Teams have conceded just one goal in their Champions League group matches nine times – the latest was Monaco in the 2014-15 season. Benfica's Anderson Talisca was the only player to score against Monaco's rock-solid defence.

Goalscoring keeper

Goalkeepers occasionally score goals, but only one goalkeeper has scored more than once in the Champions League. Hans Jörg Butt scored three penalties, each for a different German team (Hamburg in 2000, Bayer Leverkusen in 2002 and Bayern Munich in 2009) and each time against Juventus!

Hans Jörg Butt confidently scores a penalty and the first of Bayern's four goals against Juventus in a 2009-10 Group A match.

Keeping it clean

German goalkeeper Jens Lehmann holds the record for the most clean sheets in a row in the Champions League. He did not concede a goal in ten games for Arsenal in the 2005-06 and 2006-07 seasons, a total run of 853 minutes.

Defensive lynchpins

Paolo Maldini played more Champions League matches than any other defender – a record 139. Close behind him are Roberto Carlos on 128 appearances and Carles Puyol on 120. Maldini won the competition five times with AC Milan (1988-89, 1989-90, 1993-94, 2002-03, 2006-07).

Clean-sheet kings

Edwin van der Sar was the first goalkeeper to record 50 clean sheets in the Champions League. The Ajax, Juventus and Manchester United keeper reached a total of 51 clean sheets before retiring in 2011. Real Madrid goalkeeper Iker Casillas tops the chart with 52.

HOME AND away

Buoyed by a familiar stadium packed with raucous home fans cheering them on, many teams in the Champions League perform at their best at home. They sometimes go on a long unbeaten run or overturn tough odds to triumph in the home leg of a knockout round.

Bremen bounce back

After going two goals down to Anderlecht, Werder Bremen (in green above) faced a thrashing in the 1993-94 Champions League group stage. But with most of the 32,000 fans at their Weserstadion roaring them on, Bremen scored five times in the last 25 minutes to win 5-3.

Real's German hoodoo

Real Madrid have an extraordinarily bad record when playing away in Germany. The Spanish giants have played clubs in Germany 25 times in European competitions and won only once. Amongst their worst results was a 5-1 mauling by Hamburg in the 1979-80 European Cup.

A dejected Cristiano Ronaldo after Real's 2-1 defeat to Borussia Dortmund in October 2012.

Spanish fortress

The Santiago Bernabéu Stadium is the home of Real Madrid. From April 2011 to March 2015, fans went 21 games without seeing a Champions League defeat at home. What's more, Real scored 66 goals in those 21 games.

Bayern Munich celebrate their crucial second goal, scored in the 88th minute by Thomas Müller, at Arsenal's Emirates Stadium in 2014.

Home advantage

Saint-Étienne lost the first leg of their 1974-75 second-round knockout tie 4-1 to Hajduk Split, but won the home leg 5-1 to go through 6-5 on aggregate. Real Madrid did exactly the same against Derby County a season later.

Home from home

Sometimes teams are forced to play their 'home' games elsewhere. In 2002-03, safety concerns saw Maccabi Haifa of Israel play their home group games against Olympiacos, Bayer Leverkusen and Manchester United in Cyprus.

Away success

Ajax and Bayern Munich both hold the record for overturning home advantage and recording seven away wins in a row. Ajax's run lasted from 1995 to 1997, while Bayern's began and ended with wins over Arsenal at the Emirates Stadium in 2013 and 2014.

MAGIC
moments

Super skills and moments of outrageous vision or technique light up Champions League games each season. Sometimes an amazing dribble, sensational goal or acrobatic save remains in the memory for many years afterwards.

Zinedine Zidane prepares to strike the winning goal in the 2002 Champions League final.

Dejan's stunner

In their 2010-11 Champions League quarter-final against FC Schalke 04, Internazionale's Dejan Stanković struck an incredible volley straight into the net from one metre past the halfway line. It was Stanković's first touch of the ball, as the match had begun just 25 seconds earlier.

Victory volley

French maestro Zinedine Zidane scored with an unstoppable shot for Real Madrid in the 2001-02 Champions League final against Bayer Leverkusen. Showing perfect technique, the three-times FIFA World Player of the Year struck a majestic volley that gave Hans Jörg Butt no chance. It proved to be the winning goal.

Great saves

Oliver Kahn wrote himself into Bayern Munich folklore with a stunning performance in the 2000-01 final. Facing Valencia, Kahn made three spectacular penalty shootout saves from Zlatko Zahović, Amedeo Carboni and Mauricio Pellegrino. Kahn won the man of the match award and helped Bayern scoop their fourth trophy.

Real Madrid's Ivan Helguera flinches as Juventus striker David Trezeguet scores with a brilliant overhead kick in the 2004-05 tournament.

Brilliant Bressan

Mauro Bressan was a journeyman midfielder who played in various leagues in Italy and Switzerland. He played only three Champions League games for Fiorentina, but against Barcelona in 1999 he scored a spectacular overhead kick from well outside the penalty area. Bressan also produced an elegant back-heeled pass for a team-mate to score in the same game.

Lionel Messi celebrates his 2011 semi-final wonder goal.

Magical Messi

Lionel Messi frequently lights up Champions League matches for Barcelona, but he surpassed himself in the 2010-11 semi-final against Real Madrid. Messi collected the ball near the centre circle, weaved his way past four challenges and scored with a right-foot shot to take Barcelona into the final.

LAST-GASP goals

Borussia Dortmund needed to beat Marseille to qualify for the 2013-14 Round of 16 stage. With just three minutes to go before full-time, Kevin Großkreutz became their hero when his shot found the back of the net. His strike was just one of a number of last-gasp goals in the Champions League that have proved crucial.

Kevin Großkreutz, playing as a full back, celebrates his memorable strike against Marseille.

Goalkeeper's goal

In the 94th minute of a 2009-10 Group H match, Standard Liège's goalkeeper Sinan Bolat came up for an attacking free kick and powered a bullet header into AZ Alkmaar's goal. The goal saw Standard Liège move from fourth to third in the group and enabled them to qualify for the Europa League.

Squeaking through

Newcastle United's 2002-03 Champions League campaign began disastrously with three defeats in a row. At 2-2 in their last group game against Feyenoord, they faced an early exit from the competition until, in the 91st minute, Craig Bellamy popped up to score the winner and see Newcastle progress.

Dortmund double

Borussia Dortmund scored two injury-time goals to turn their 2012-13 Champions League quarter-final against Malaga from defeat into victory. First, Marco Reus struck in the 91st minute, before Felipe Santana scored in the 93rd and last minute of the match.

Bailing out Barça

Down to ten men and trailing to a Michael Essien goal, Barcelona were in deep trouble in the 2008-09 Champions League semi-final against Chelsea. In the 93rd minute, Lionel Messi squared the ball to Andrés Iniesta just outside the penalty area, who struck a sweet shot past Petr Čech. Barcelona went through on away goals and then won the final.

Andrés Iniesta (right) and Samuel Eto'o roar with delight at Iniesta's last-gasp goal against Chelsea that took Barcelona into the 2009 final.

Favourites' final flourish

Favourites Bayern Munich were trailing 1-0 with less than 30 seconds of extra time to go in the 1974 European Cup final, when Hans-Georg Schwarzenbeck rifled in a long-range shot to take the tie into a replay. Bayern won the repeat comfortably. Forty years later, Real Madrid's Sergio Ramos (left) equalised in the 93rd minute of the 2014 final. The runners-up in both of those matches were Atlético Madrid.

PENALTY
shootouts

Penalty shootouts were introduced to the European Cup in the 1970-71 season. They are used to determine the outcome if the scores are tied after extra time. Teams each take five penalties and then further rounds of sudden-death penalties if the scores are still tied. Shootouts have resulted in some nail-biting experiences for both players and fans.

First miss

The first penalty shootout in the European Cup was in the second round of the 1970-71 competition, when Everton and Borussia Mönchengladbach were tied after extra time. Everton's Joe Royle became the first player to miss a penalty in a European Cup shootout, but his side went through, winning 4-3.

AC Milan's Andriy Shevchenko scored the winning penalty in the 2003 final versus Juventus.

Manuel Neuer saves a Real Madrid penalty in the 2012 semi. He also saved a penalty and scored one in the 2012 final shootout against Chelsea.

Diving Duckadam

An astonishing display by Steaua Bucharest's goalkeeper Helmuth Duckadam occurred in the 1986 European Cup final shootout. Duckadam saved all four of Barcelona's penalties to see Steaua become the first Romanian club to win the competition.

Chelsea slip up

In the 2008 final shootout, with the score at 4-3, John Terry's penalty would have made Chelsea champions. But Terry slipped as he took it, the ball hit the post and Chelsea's opponents Manchester United came back to win 6-5.

Marvellous Manuel

After a 2-1 second-leg win saw the scores tied at 3-3 on aggregate, Real Madrid and Bayern Munich took part in a nerve-shredding 2011-12 semi-final shootout. Madrid scored just one of their penalties, as Bayern keeper Manuel Neuer made two saves to deny Cristiano Ronaldo and Kaká, who were the two most-expensive players in the world at the time.

Cosmic Cosmin

Ludogorets Razgrad's goalkeeper was sent off just a minute before the end of extra time in their final qualifying game of the 2014-15 Champions League. Central defender Cosmin Moti went in goal for the penalty shootout and scored Ludogorets' first penalty. While in goal, he saved two of Steaua Bucharest's penalties to propel his team into the 2014-15 Champions League group stages for the very first time.

MATCH
officials

Every Champions League game is run by a team of match officials. These officials, including the referee and his two assistants that run the line, are often at the centre of the action and drama.

Elite referees

Champions League games are run by UEFA's elite referees. The pace of modern football demands that officials are extremely fit – in a typical Champions League match the referee may run more than 10km to keep up with play. Elite referees have to retire at the end of the season in which they reach the age of 45.

Three of each

Referee Wolfgang Stark (left) had a busy night in a 2013-14 Champions League Group C game, when he sent off three Anderlecht players and awarded three penalties to their opponents, Olympiacos. Despite missing two, the Greek side ran out 3-1 winners.

MOST CHAMPIONS LEAGUE MATCHES REFEREED (1992-93 TO 2014-15)

- **53** Kim Milton Nielsen (Denmark)
- **51** Wolfgang Stark (Germany)
- **50** Ľuboš Michel (Slovakia)
- **48** Markus Merk (Germany)
- **47** Terje Hauge (Norway)
- **46** Frank de Bleeckere (Belgium)
- **45** Anders Frisk (Sweden)
- **42** Urs Meier (Switzerland)
- **41** Kyros Vassaras (Greece)
- **40** Manuel Mejuto González (Spain)

Kim Milton Neilsen refereed one Champions League final – Porto's 3-0 victory over AS Monaco in 2003-04.

Carlos Velasco Carballo uses vanishing spray during a group G match between FC Schalke 04 and NK Maribor in September 2014.

Final refs

Englishman Arthur Ellis refereed the first European Cup final in 1956. Since then, only four referees have taken charge of two finals: Leo Horn (1957 and 1962), Gottfried Dienst (1961 and 1965), Concetto lo Bello (1968 and 1970) and Károly Palotai (1976 and 1981).

Vanishing spray

As the Champions League has grown, the pressure on referees to make correct decisions has increased. Several aids have been introduced, including goal-line officials and, since the 2014-15 season, vanishing spray. Referees use the spray to mark a white, foamy line at free kicks so that the defensive wall does not encroach on the 10-yard (9.1-m) distance between them and the free-kick taker.

REDS AND yellows

The referee in every match can issue cards for fouls or infringements of football's Laws of the Game. Two yellow cards, or a straight red for a serious foul or other offence, sees a player sent off and his team left to struggle on with ten men.

Vieira sees red

When Internazionale's French midfielder Patrick Viera was sent off in 2006, it left him with an unwanted record. He remains the only player to have been sent off in the Champions League for three different teams – the others being Arsenal and Juventus.

First in a final

The first player to be shown a red card in a final was Arsenal keeper Jens Lehmann (left), in 2006. The first Norwegian to referee a final, Terje Hauge, sent him off in the 18th minute for a foul outside the penalty area on Barcelona's Samuel Eto'o. Two years later, the second red card in a final was shown to Chelsea's Didier Drogba in the 117th minute.

In the book

Paul Scholes collected more yellow cards than any other player in the Champions League. The Manchester United midfielder was booked 32 times. Two players have been sent off four times in the Champions League – Edgar Davids and Zlatan Ibrahimović.

Bad discipline

Viera's red card is one of 20 that Juventus players have been shown in the Champions League – more than any other club. Internazionale (17) and Galatasaray (15) are close behind. Ten of Juventus' red cards were picked up in just two seasons (2000-01 and 2005-06).

Juventus midfielder Pavel Nedved (above) is sent off against Arsenal in the 2005-06 quarter-final.

Speedy sending off

In March 2015, Shakhtar Donetsk defender Oleksandr Kucher was sent off after just three minutes, 59 seconds in a Round of 16 match against Bayern Munich for a foul on Mario Götze (below). The Champions League's fastest ever red card sparked a terrible night for Shakhtar, who were thrashed 7-0 by Bayern.

Part 4:
Great Players

Many of the world's very best players have graced the European Cup and Champions League over the years, including super stopper Manuel Neuer, the mesmerising Lionel Messi and the sumptuously skilled Cristiano Ronaldo.

While the cream of Europe's footballing talent is often on display, some of the competition's biggest stars have come from outside Europe. One of the first was Alfredo di Stéfano, an Argentinian who was an attacking lynchpin in the Real Madrid side of the 1950s. He was followed by stellar South Americans such as Diego Maradona and Luis Suárez as well as amazing African players including Didier Drogba and Samuel Eto'o.

The 2014 World Footballer of the Year, Cristiano Ronaldo, shoots past the planet's best goalkeeper, Manuel Neuer. The occasion is the second leg of the 2013-14 semi-final between Bayern Munich and Real Madrid, a game in which Ronaldo took his season's tally to 16 goals. His 17th, in the final, set a Champions League/European Cup record.

GOALKEEPERS

Petr Čech

Date of birth: **20 May 1982** / Nationality: **Czech**
Major clubs: **Sparta Prague, Chelsea**

After moving to Chelsea in 2004 from French club Rennes, Čech spent almost a decade as the Blues' number one until the emergence of Thibaut Courtois in 2014. Easily identified by the protective headguard he wears following a fractured skull in 2006, Čech has played more than 100 Champions League games and appeared in two finals, winning in 2012. He has also won UEFA's club goalkeeper of the year award three times.

Manuel Neuer

Date of birth: **27 March 1986**
Nationality: **German**
Major clubs: **Schalke 04, Bayern Munich**

Confident and agile, Neuer often leaves his penalty area to snuff out opposition attacks. His shot-stopping prowess helped Schalke 04 to the 2010-11 semi-finals, after which he moved to Bayern Munich. Neuer has reached two Champions League finals with Bayern, losing the first to Chelsea but starring in their win over Borussia Dortmund in 2013. The following year, he won the FIFA World Cup with Germany and was voted the world's best goalkeeper.

Petr Čech saved two penalties during the 2012 final shootout, from Bayern Munich's Ivica Olić and Bastian Schweinsteiger.

Edwin van der Sar

Date of birth: **29 October 1970**
Nationality: **Dutch**
Major clubs: **Ajax, Juventus, Manchester United**

Edwin van der Sar won his first Champions League with Ajax in 1995 and his second with Manchester United 13 years later – the longest gap for a player between victories. He was capped 130 times for the Dutch national side, but a third tilt at European glory proved elusive when Manchester United reached the 2011 Champions League final. The 3-1 defeat to Barcelona was his last professional match before he retired.

Iker Casillas

Date of birth: **20 May 1981** / **Nationality:** **Spanish**
Major clubs: **Real Madrid**

In 2000, at age 19, Real Madrid's Casillas became the youngest goalkeeper to appear in a Champions League final. In the 2002 final he came on as a sub in the 68th minute, after César Sánchez left the field with a leg injury. Casillas then pulled off a string of breathtaking saves to help the Spanish giants to their ninth European triumph. One of the best European keepers of the 2000s, Casillas captained Real to their tenth title in 2014 and has kept a record 52 clean sheets.

GOALKEEPERS

Gianluigi Buffon

Date of birth: **28 January 1978**
Nationality: **Italian**
Major clubs: **Parma, Juventus**

As the world's most expensive goalkeeper when he moved to Juventus in 2001 (a record that still stands), Buffon proved to be a shrewd investment. An almost constant presence in the Juve goal, he has played in more than 500 Italian league matches and won the Serie A goalkeeper award a record nine times. A frequent star in Juventus' Champions League performances, Buffon is yet to win the trophy, although he reached the final back in 2002-03 and again in 2014-15.

Victor Valdés

Date of birth: **14 January 1982** / Nationality: **Spanish**
Major clubs: **Barcelona, Manchester United**

Valdés has been denied many Spanish caps by the excellent Iker Casillas, but he boasts a superior Champions League record to his countryman, having won the title three times with Barcelona. The first was in 2006, when he produced some crucial saves against Arsenal. In 2007, he broke Barcelona's record for the most minutes (466) without conceding a goal in European competition and enjoyed further Champions League success in 2009 and 2011.

Oliver Kahn

Date of birth: **15 June 1969** / Nationality: **German**
Major clubs: **Bayern Munich**

Few keepers were more feared in one-on-one situations than Bayern Munich's mighty stopper. Kahn played more than 100 Champions League games and was voted the Bundesliga's best keeper on seven separate occasions. Bitterly disappointed with a runners-up medal in 1999, he bounced back two seasons later, making three penalty-shootout saves to help Bayern secure their first Champions League or European Cup triumph for 25 years.

Oliver Kahn celebrates as Bayern beat Real Madrid in 2007. In the same year he played in his 535th Bundesliga match – a record.

Peter Schmeichel

Date of birth:
18 November 1963
Nationality: **Danish**
Major clubs: **Brøndby, Manchester United, Sporting Clube de Portugal**

Bought by Manchester United for less than £550,000, Schmeichel became one of the very best keepers of the 1990s. His commanding size and presence prevented many goals and in 1999 helped United to their first European triumph in 30 years. In total, he played 43 European matches for United.

Paolo Maldini

Date of birth: **26 June 1968** / Nationality: **Italian**
Major clubs: **AC Milan**

Maldini is a five-time European Cup / Champions League winner and one of the few players to have won in three different decades. He spent an incredible 25 seasons with AC Milan, playing 139 games in the competition. Maldini was a brilliant, athletic defender, able to play as a full back or central defender. His goal after 52 seconds in the 2005 Champions League final remains the fastest scored in a final and made him the oldest final goalscorer.

Philipp Lahm

Date of birth: **11 November 1983**
Nationality: **German**
Major clubs: **Bayern Munich**

Lahm is one of the world's most skilful and intelligent defenders. He spent most of his early and mid-career as a full back, but has recently appeared for Bayern in midfield, where his vision can turn defence into attack. A World Cup winner with Germany and seven-time Bundesliga winner with Bayern, Lahm has played more than 90 Champions League games for the Munich team, acquiring two runners-up and one winner's medal.

Lahm's enduring excellence has seen him make UEFA Team of the Year five times (2006, 2008, 2012, 2013 and 2014).

Diego Godín

Date of birth: **16 February 1986** / Nationality: **Uruguayan**
Major clubs: **Villarreal, Atlético Madrid**

A skilful and dominating central defender who is an excellent organiser, Godín is a veteran of two World Cups with Uruguay. He proved himself a key part of the Atlético defence that won La Liga and reached the final of the 2013-14 Champions League. Although he scored in the final, Real Madrid triumphed and Godín had to be content with a runners-up medal.

Carles Puyol

Date of birth: **13 April 1978** / Nationality: **Spanish**
Major clubs: **Barcelona**

Strong, tough-tackling and aggressive, Puyol started as a goalkeeper and then a striker at his local club Pobla de Segur, before joining Barcelona's youth system aged 16. He spent the whole of his career at the Spanish giants and was captain for ten years, winning six La Liga titles and enjoying three Champions League successes – in 2006, 2009 and 2011.

Raphaël Varane

Date of birth: **25 April 1993**
Nationality: **French**
Major clubs: **Lens, Real Madrid**

One of the hottest defensive prospects in European football, Varane was just 21 when he played all 120 minutes of the 2013-14 Champions League final against Atlético Madrid. A quick, mobile central defender, Varane remains a transfer target for other top Champions League sides, even though he has signed a contract to keep him at Real Madrid until 2020.

DEFENDERS

Thiago Silva

Date of birth: **22 September 1984**
Nationality: **Brazilian**
Major clubs: **Fluminense, AC Milan, Paris Saint-Germain**

Silva started out as a winger, converted to a defender and played all over Europe before Paris Saint-Germain paid more than 36 million Euros to bring him to France. He is a strong tackler, good in the air and an excellent reader of a game who often gets into position early to stop opposing attacks. Although he has won the Italian and French league titles with his clubs, Champions League glory has so far eluded him.

Franz Beckenbauer

Date of birth: **11 September 1945**
Nationality: **German**
Major clubs: **Bayern Munich, SV Hamburg**

Beckenbauer was an elegant, highly skilled defender. He started out as a midfielder, but revolutionized football tactics when he moved to sweeper. Instead of playing behind the defence, Beckenbauer would move forwards with the ball, linking defence and attack with his incisive passing. Making his Bayern debut back in 1964, he would go on to captain the club to three European Cups in a row in the mid-1970s.

Thiago Silva and John Terry tussle during their 2014-15 quarter-final. Silva saw PSG through with a thumping 114th-minute headed goal.

Gerard Piqué

Date of birth: **2 February 1987** / Nationality: **Spanish**
Major clubs: **Manchester United, Barcelona**

Piqué rejoined Barcelona after a spell at Manchester United, during which he won the 2007-08 Champions League despite not playing in the final. Seven of his nine Champions League goals have come for Barcelona, with whom he won further titles in 2009, 2011 and 2015. Piqué uses his pace and superb reading of the game to break up opponents' attacks.

John Terry

Date of birth: **7 December 1980** / Nationality: **English**
Major clubs: **Chelsea**

Strong in the air and rock-solid on the ground, Terry is an attacking threat from corners and free kicks. A slip in the 2007-08 final penalty shootout cost Chelsea the trophy, but four years later Terry's performances helped take his team to the final. The Blues lifted the trophy without Terry, as he had been sent off in the semi-final victory over Barcelona. In October 2014, he played his 100th Champions League match.

Mats Hummels

Date of birth: **16 December 1988**
Nationality: **German**
Major clubs: **Borussia Dortmund**

Mature beyond his years, Hummels has formed a powerful partnership with Neven Subotić in Dortmund's central defence. A product of the Bayern Munich academy, he signed for Dortmund in 2009 and is now captain of the club. He led them to the 2012-13 Champions League final, which followed a Bundesliga and DFB-Pokal Cup double the previous season.

Thomas Müller

Date of birth: **13 September 1989**
Nationality: **German**
Major clubs: **Bayern Munich**

Müller scored in his very first Champions League game, adding the last goal in Bayern's 7-1 thrashing of Sporting Clube de Portugal in 2009. A powerful runner and an attacking force, he has twice been a runner-up in the Champions League (in 2010 and 2012). He had an epic 2012-13 season, scoring 23 goals from midfield, including eight in the Champions League, as Bayern won the competition along with the Bundesliga and DFB-Pokal Cup.

Ryan Giggs

Date of birth: **29 November 1973**
Nationality: **Welsh**
Major clubs: **Manchester United**

Giggs made his Champions League debut in September 1993 and was still playing 20 years later. A terrific winger with pace and great dribbling skills, Giggs reached four Champions League finals with Manchester United, winning two and notching up an astonishing 151 Champions League matches. He is also the only player to have scored in 16 different Champions League seasons, striking 30 goals in total.

Andrés Iniesta

Date of birth: **11 May 1984** / Nationality: **Spanish**
Major clubs: **Barcelona**

The scorer of the goal that won Spain the 2010 FIFA World Cup, Iniesta has starred in a stellar Barcelona midfield where he built up a brilliant understanding with fellow midfielder Xavi Hernández. Iniesta specializes in attacking runs where his pace and vision allow him to score goals or provide assists.

Selected four times for UEFA Team of the Year, he has won four Champions League finals with Barcelona (2006, 2009, 2011, 2015).

Thomas Müller and Andrés Iniesta compete during the 2013 semi-final. Müller scored two goals as Bayern defeated Barcelona 4-0.

MOST CHAMPIONS LEAGUE APPEARANCES
(INCLUDING QUALIFYING)

157	Xavi Hernández
152	Iker Casillas
151	Ryan Giggs
144	Raúl González
139	Paolo Maldini
131	Clarence Seedorf
130	Paul Scholes
128	Roberto Carlos
120	Carles Puyol
119	Cristiano Ronaldo

Clarence Seedorf

Date of birth: **1 April 1976**
Nationality: **Dutch/Surinamese**
Major clubs: **Ajax, Sampdoria, Real Madrid, Internazionale, AC Milan**

Seedorf was Ajax's youngest player when he debuted at age 16. Less than three years later he was a Champions League winner, playing in the 1995 final against AC Milan, a club he would join in 2002 and win the Champions League with (in 2003 and 2007). A complete midfielder, able to shoot from distance, tackle and pass, Seedorf also won the competition with Real Madrid in 1998, making him the only player to triumph with three different clubs.

MIDFIELDERS

Andrea Pirlo

Date of birth:
19 May 1979
Nationality:
Italian
Major clubs:
**Internazionale,
AC Milan,
Juventus**

The veteran playmaker has long graced the Champions League with his eye for space and a precision pass, either short or long. In more than 110 Champions League appearances, Pirlo has twice won the tournament with AC Milan (2003, 2007) and helped Juventus, whom he joined in 2011, to a runners-up spot in 2014-15.

Johan Cruyff

Date of birth: **25 April 1947**
Nationality: **Dutch**
Major clubs: **Ajax, Barcelona**

A master of movement and control, Cruyff often played in attack, but in many games he was found all over the pitch. His passing and understanding of space put him ahead of his rivals. As part of the Ajax side that swept all before them at the start of the 1970s, Cruyff won three European Cups with the Dutch club and a further one as manager of Barcelona in 1992.

Xavi and Paul Scholes have played over 280 Champions League matches between them – more than many clubs.

Xavi Hernández

Date of birth: **25 January 1980**
Nationality: **Spanish** / Major clubs: **Barcelona**

Xavi joined the Barcelona youth system way back in 1991 and won eight La Liga titles with the Spanish club. His passing, vision and ability to find space in even the most crowded areas of the pitch allowed him to control games and earned him the Man of the Match award in the 2009 Champions League final – one of four Champions League successes Xavi has enjoyed, including victory in the 2014-15 final, his very last game for Barcelona.

Paul Scholes

Date of birth: **16 November 1974** / Nationality: **English**
Major clubs: **Manchester United**

Scholes played for one club – Manchester United – where he won 11 English Premier League titles and two Champions Leagues between 1991 and 2013. He was a highly accurate passer, able to dictate the flow of a game and was considered one of the best midfielders in Europe. The occasional poor tackle lead to a record 32 yellow cards in the Champions League, but he also scored 24 Champions League goals (one of the highest totals for a midfielder).

MIDFIELDERS

Zinedine Zidane

Date of birth: **23 June 1972**
Nationality: **French**
Major clubs: **Bordeaux, Juventus, Real Madrid**

One of the best technical midfielders of all time, Zidane could pass, dribble, shoot and score headers, all with devastating ease. After losing two Champions League finals with Juventus, Zidane moved to Real Madrid in 2001 for a world-record fee and made an instant impact. In the 2002 Champions League final, he scored the winning goal – an outstanding volley from a high, hanging ball that is rated as one of the greatest ever Champions League goals.

Arjen Robben

Date of birth: **23 January 1984** / Nationality: **Dutch**
Major clubs: **PSV Eindhoven, Chelsea, Real Madrid, Bayern Munich**

A nightmare for defenders to mark, Robben is a winger with the ability to beat a man and deliver a highly accurate cross or shot. His attacking flair and will to win have made him part of league-winning teams in four different countries, as well as a Champions League winner in 2013, a game in which he was man of the match.

Toni Kroos made more successful passes than any other player in the 2013-14 Champions League – 1,059, a success rate of 94 per cent.

Toni Kroos

Date of birth: **4 January 1990**
Nationality: **German** / Major clubs: **Bayern Munich, Real Madrid**

Kroos debuted for the Bayern first team at the age of 17. He is a central midfielder with a wide range of passes that he frequently uses to unlock defences. He starred in Bayern's run to the 2012 Champions League final and was prominent in the following campaign until a leg injury in the quarter-finals ended his season early. In 2014, he won the FIFA World Cup and in the same year moved to Real Madrid in a deal worth more than 25 million Euros.

Eden Hazard was France's youngest ever Player of the Year in 2011. He retained his title in 2012 before moving to Chelsea.

Eden Hazard

Date of birth:
7 January 1991
Nationality: **Belgian**
Major clubs: **Lille, Chelsea**

Hazard is a highly creative and, at times, explosive attacking force. He can play wide or through the middle of the pitch, where his balance, ball control and skill allow him to weave through a packed defence or bend a curling shot out of the keeper's reach. He joined Chelsea in 2012 and by the end of 2014-15 had scored over 40 goals from midfield for the club, including three in the 2014-15 Champions League.

MIDFIELDERS

James Rodríguez

Date of birth: **12 July 1991**
Nationality: **Colombian**
Major clubs: **Porto, Monaco, Real Madrid**

One of the brightest stars in world football, Rodríguez set the 2014 FIFA World Cup alight with his sensational attacking play, including the goal of the tournament, a powerful volley against Uruguay. After playing in Europe for Porto and Monaco, he joined Real Madrid in 2014 and scored on his Champions League debut for Real against FC Basel.

Flying wingers Gareth Bale and Franck Ribéry chase down the ball during their 2013-14 Champions League semi-final.

Mesut Özil

Date of birth: **15 October 1988**
Nationality: **German**
Major clubs: **Schalke 04, Werder Bremen, Real Madrid, Arsenal**

Özil is a skilful attacking midfielder who spent five years in the youth set-up of German club Rot-Weiss Essen. In 2013 he became the most expensive German footballer ever, when he transferred to Arsenal from Real Madrid for a fee of around 50 million Euros. He is particularly adept at providing the crucial pass for others to score and between 2009-10 and 2013-14 made more assists – 69 – than any other player in the top leagues of Europe.

Gareth Bale

Date of birth: **16 July 1989**
Nationality: **Welsh**
Major clubs: **Tottenham Hotspur, Real Madrid**

Bale's unbelievable pace and trickery on the ball see him race past defenders, while he also has a devastating left-footed shot. He scored his first ever hat-trick in professional football in the 2010-11 Champions League against the reigning champions, Internazionale. In 2013 he moved to Real Madrid, where he scored 22 goals in the season. Six of these came in the Champions League, including a goal in the final, the first ever by a Welsh player.

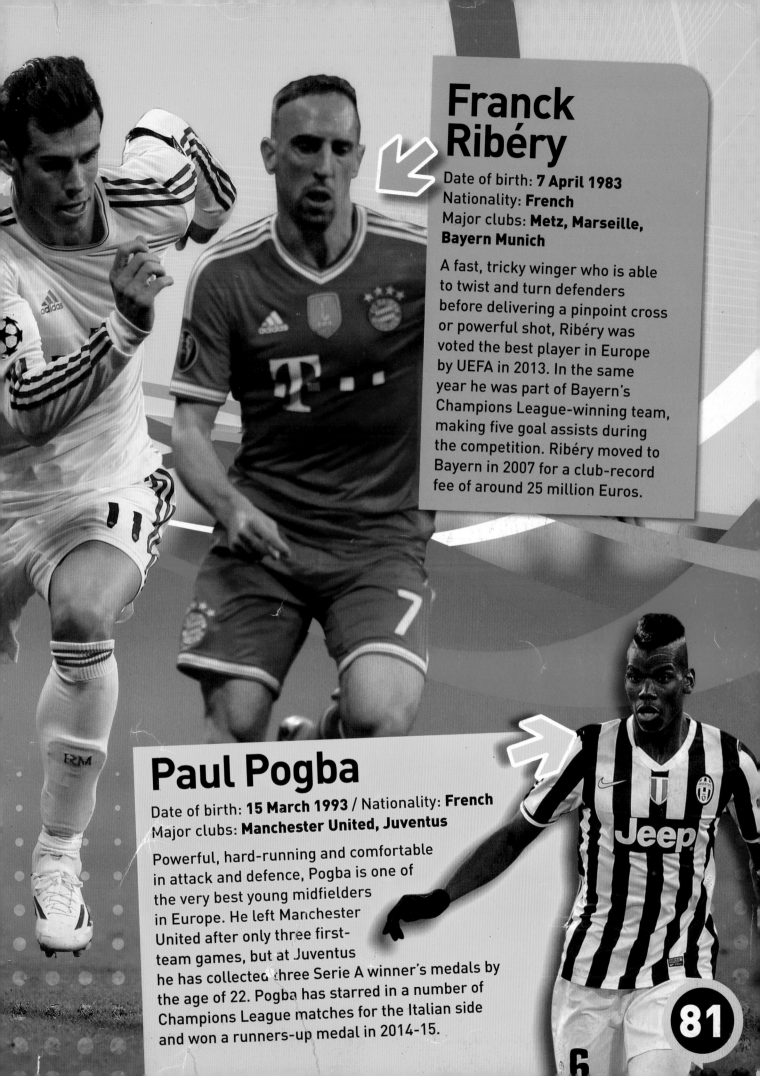

Franck Ribéry

Date of birth: **7 April 1983**
Nationality: **French**
Major clubs: **Metz, Marseille, Bayern Munich**

A fast, tricky winger who is able to twist and turn defenders before delivering a pinpoint cross or powerful shot, Ribéry was voted the best player in Europe by UEFA in 2013. In the same year he was part of Bayern's Champions League-winning team, making five goal assists during the competition. Ribéry moved to Bayern in 2007 for a club-record fee of around 25 million Euros.

Paul Pogba

Date of birth: **15 March 1993** / Nationality: **French**
Major clubs: **Manchester United, Juventus**

Powerful, hard-running and comfortable in attack and defence, Pogba is one of the very best young midfielders in Europe. He left Manchester United after only three first-team games, but at Juventus he has collected three Serie A winner's medals by the age of 22. Pogba has starred in a number of Champions League matches for the Italian side and won a runners-up medal in 2014-15.

81

Zlatan Ibrahimović poses after scoring against Dynamo Kiev. His man-of-the-match performance inspired the French club to a 4-1 victory.

Zlatan makes it six

The much-travelled Swedish striker Zlatan Ibrahimović made history on 18 September 2012. After Dynamo Kiev's Taras Mikhalik had given away a penalty in their group game against Paris Saint-Germain, Ibrahimović stepped up to convert the penalty past Maksym Koval. The goal made Ibrahimović the first player in Champions League history to score for six different clubs. His first Champions League goal had come ten years and one day earlier, when he struck twice on his tournament debut for Ajax against French champions Lyon. The maverick striker went on to score for Juventus, Internazionale, Barcelona and AC Milan. In 2013-14, Ibrahimović scored four goals in one game, as PSG beat Belgian side Anderlecht 5-0 to record their biggest away win in Europe.

ATTACKERS

Thierry Henry

Date of birth: **17 August 1977** / Nationality: **French**
Major clubs: **Monaco, Arsenal, Barcelona**

Henry started out at Monaco as a winger, but became a graceful and skilful striker with an eye for the unexpected under manager Arsène Wenger at Arsenal. Joining the London club in 1999, he broke their all-time goalscoring record in 2005 with two goals against Sparta Prague in the Champions League. In 2007, he moved to Barcelona, where he won two Spanish league titles and the 2008-09 Champions League.

Edinson Cavani's header against Chelsea in the 2014-15 Round of 16 took his tally to 15 goals in 30 Champions League games.

Edinson Cavani

Date of birth: **14 February 1987**
Nationality: **Uruguayan**
Major clubs: **Palermo, Napoli, Paris Saint-Germain**

Cavani moved to Palermo as a 19-year-old, then switched to Napoli where he scored over 100 goals in less than 140 appearances – a startling return. A desire to play in the Champions League saw him move to Paris Saint-Germain in 2013. After scoring 20 goals in just six months of his first season at PSG, he netted five in the six 2014-15 Champions League group games, including the winning goal after 56 seconds against APOEL Nicosia.

Gerd Müller

Date of birth: **3 November 1945**
Nationality: **German**
Major clubs: **Bayern Munich**

A record 68 goals in 62 matches for West Germany – and an equally impressive 365 goals in 427 league matches for Bayern Munich – make it clear that Müller was a goalscoring machine. The winner of three European Cups with Bayern, Müller was superb in the air and had an incredibly powerful shot. His goal-a-game record in the European Cup (scoring 35 goals in as many matches) is unlikely to be bettered.

Francisco Gento

Date of birth: **21 October 1933**
Nationality: **Spanish**
Major clubs: **Racing de Santander, Real Madrid**

Gento was a quick forward who played out wide or through the centre of the pitch. Joining Real Madrid in 1953, he didn't leave the club until 1971, appearing in an unrivalled eight European Cup finals along the way and winning six – a record to this day. Gento scored in every European Cup season until 1966-67, hitting a total of 30 goals.

Wayne Rooney

Date of birth: **24 October 1985** / Nationality: **English**
Major clubs: **Everton, Manchester United**

Rooney announced himself on the European stage with a hat-trick on his Champions League debut for Manchester United against Fenerbahçe in 2004. He was just 18 years old. The most technically gifted English striker of his generation, Rooney can drop back into midfield to link attacks or lead the line, scoring explosive and spectacular goals. He has struck over 200 goals for United, including 30 in the Champions League, and he won the competition in 2008.

ATTACKERS

Raúl González

Date of birth: **27 June 1977**
Nationality: **Spanish**
Major clubs: **Real Madrid, Schalke 04**

Raúl moved to Real Madrid from Atlético Madrid as a youth player. He became a lethal finisher for the Spanish giants, scoring 323 goals in all competitions and was the top scorer in the Champions League twice (1999-2000, 2000-01). He netted a record 66 times for Real Madrid in the competition and won three Champions Leagues before moving to Schalke 04 in 2010. There, he scored a further five Champions League goals to bring his tally up to 71 and help the club reach the semis in 2010-11 for the first time in their history.

> Samuel Eto'o's 33 Champions League goals have come for five different clubs and include strikes in the 2006 and 2009 finals.

Robert Lewandowski

Date of birth: **21 August 1988** / Nationality: **Polish**
Major clubs: **Lech Poznań, Borussia Dortmund, Bayern Munich**

The free-scoring Polish striker is superb at timing runs to finish off his team's attacking moves. He scored 10 goals in 13 Champions League games as Dortmund reached the 2013 final, including his four-goal trouncing of Real Madrid – the first time a player has scored four goals in a semi-final. The following season he struck six times in eight games, before moving in the summer to German rivals Bayern Munich on a free transfer.

QUICKEST STRIKERS TO REACH 50 GOALS

Ruud van Nistelrooy
62 games
Lionel Messi
66 games
Cristiano Ronaldo
91 games
Raúl González
97 games
Thierry Henry
103 games

Lionel Messi

Date of birth: **24 June 1987**
Nationality: **Argentinian** / Major clubs: **Barcelona**

The four-time FIFA World Player of the Year/Ballon d'Or winner has been lighting up Europe since he scored his first Champions League goal against Panathinaikos in 2005. His quick feet and reactions, mesmerising skill and vision see him weave past opponents to score against even the meanest defences. In 2012, he scored an unbelievable 91 goals for club and country, including five in a single Champions League game against Bayer Leverkusen. Messi has scored 77 Champions League goals, placing him second behind Cristiano Ronaldo, and has already won the competition four times.

Samuel Eto'o

Date of birth: **10 March 1981** / Nationality: **Cameroonian**
Major clubs: **Mallorca, Barcelona, Internazionale, Chelsea**

Possessing pace, power and an excellent awareness of goal, Eto'o has been an opponent's nightmare ever since he starred for Barcelona in their 2005-06 Champions League-winning season. He would enjoy a second European triumph three years later, before moving to Internazionale. There, he won the Champions League again, in 2010, becoming one of the few players to win back-to-back Champions League titles with different clubs.

ATTACKERS

Henrik Larsson

Date of birth: **20 September 1971**
Nationality: **Swedish**
Major clubs: **Feyenoord, Celtic, Barcelona**

A highly skilled, wily and electric attacker, Larsson created as many goals as he scored. His very last game for Barcelona was the 2006 Champions League final, in which he came on as a substitute and set up both of Barcelona's goals in their 2-1 victory over Arsenal. He returned to Sweden to continue playing, but had a short loan spell at Manchester United in 2007, scoring the winner in the Round of 16 game against Lille.

Sergio Agüero

Date of birth: **2 June 1988**
Nationality: **Argentinian**
Major clubs: **Independiente, Atlético Madrid, Manchester City**

A lethal marksman who can score with either foot or his head, Agüero was the youngest player to appear in the Argentinian league when he debuted for Independiente aged just 15 years, 35 days. After moving to Europe, his 19 La Liga goals in 2007-08 propelled Atlético Madrid into the Champions League for the first time since 1996-97. He has since won two English Premier League titles with Manchester City but is still chasing a Champions League prize.

Mario Mandžukić

Date of birth: **21 May 1986**
Nationality: **Croatian**
Major clubs: **Dinamo Zagreb, Bayern Munich, Atlético Madrid**

Mandžukić is an energetic striker with the stamina to run all game long and the strength to hold off opponents. He has a very good eye for goal, scoring more than 20 goals a season for two seasons both at Dinamo Zagreb and Bayern Munich, with whom he won the Champions League in 2013. Transferred to Atletico Madrid for the 2014-15 season, Mandžukić scored his first hat-trick for the club in the Champions League against Olympiacos.

Neymar

Date of birth: **5 February 1992** / Nationality: **Brazilian**
Major clubs: **Santos, Barcelona**

Explosive, pacy and a strong dribbler, Neymar is an idol to Brazilian fans, for whom he has already scored 43 goals in his first 62 international games. Following a move to Europe in 2013, he made his Champions League debut that year in Barcelona's 4-0 thrashing of Ajax. He then scored his first, second and third Champions League goals in Barca's 6-1 Group H thumping of Celtic. His last-gasp goal in the 2014-15 final sealed the trophy against Juventus.

Neymar was joint top scorer in the 2014-15 Champions League, with ten goals, including one in the final.

Karim Benzema

Date of birth: **19 December 1987** / Nationality: **French**
Major clubs: **Lyon, Real Madrid**

Benzema made his name at Lyon, where he won four French league championships before moving to Real Madrid in 2009 for around 32 million Euros. After a tough start, Benzema has flourished. In the 2013-14 season he scored five Champions League goals, including the crucial only goal of the first leg of the semi-final. He has netted 42 Champions League goals, including one in 2014 against FC Basel – Real's 1,000th goal in European competitions.

89

ATTACKERS

Luis Suárez

Date of birth: **24 January 1987**
Nationality: **Uruguayan**
Major clubs: **Ajax, Liverpool, Barcelona**

A controversial figure and a player banned after a biting incident at the 2014 FIFA World Cup, Suárez remains a sensational striker whose movement and eye for the unexpected often outwits defences. His 100th goal for Ajax was in a Champions League qualifying game and after sparking Liverpool to second in the English Premier League in 2014, he moved to Barcelona. There, he won the Champions League in his first season, scoring Barcelona's second goal in the final against Juventus.

Cristiano Ronaldo

Date of birth: **5 February 1985** / **Nationality:** **Portuguese**
Major clubs: **Manchester United, Real Madrid**

An absolute phenomenon, Ronaldo battles with Lionel Messi for the title of best player on the planet. He has searing pace, masses of trickery and a phenomenal range of wicked shots. He won the Champions League with Manchester United before moving to Real Madrid in 2009 for £80 million. By the end of 2014-15, Ronaldo had scored 313 goals for Real at a rate of more than one a game. A stellar 2013-14 season saw him score 17 Champions League goals – the most by any player in any season as Real won the competition for a record tenth time.

Marco Reus

Date of birth: 31 May 1989 / **Nationality:** German
Major clubs: Borussia Mönchengladbach, Borussia Dortmund

The German footballer of the year in 2012, Reus is known for his high work rate, skill and ability to create chances for others. He formed a potent partnership with Robert Lewandowski, which took Dortmund to the 2013 Champions League final, and ended the 2013-14 season with 23 goals and 18 assists – an excellent return.

Luis Suarez's seventh goal in the 2014-15 Champions League put Barcelona 2-1 up in the final against Juventus.

Alfredo di Stéfano

Date of birth: 4 July 1926
Nationality: Argentinian/Spanish
Major clubs: River Plate, Millonarios, Real Madrid, Espanyol

Di Stéfano was the complete attacking player. He might start the game as a central striker but would drift and sprint all over the pitch to create attacks and link play. After moving to Europe, he struck up a deadly partnership with Ferenc Puskás. They led Real Madrid through an incredible period of European dominance, winning the first five European Cups, with di Stéfano scoring in all five finals. A strike record of 49 goals in just 58 European Cup games is higher than any other leading goalscorer and testament to di Stéfano's striking prowess.

TOP SCORERS (EUROPEAN CUP AND CHAMPIONS LEAGUE, INCLUDING QUALIFYING)

Goals	Player	Appearances
78	Cristiano Ronaldo	119
77	Lionel Messi	99
71	Raúl González	144
60	Ruud van Nistelrooy	81
59	Andriy Shevchenko	116
51	Thierry Henry	115
50	Filippo Inzaghi	85
49	Alfredo di Stéfano	58
47	Eusébio	63
44	Didier Drogba	94
44	Zlatan Ibrahimović	113
44	Alessandro del Piero	92

TIMELINE

1955
The very first European Cup competition kicks off with Sporting Clube de Portugal playing Partizan Belgrade. Sporting's João Baptista Martins scores the competition's first goal in a 3-3 draw.

1956
Real Madrid beat Stade de Reims 4-3 in the first European Cup final.

1960
Real Madrid win their fifth European Cup in a row. The final, held at Hampden Park, attracts more than 127,000 spectators, the biggest European Cup or Champions League attendance ever.

1966
Ferenc Puskás becomes the oldest player to win the European Cup at the age of 39 years and 39 days.

1970
The first penalty shootout in the European Cup, between Everton and Borussia Mönchengladbach. Everton win 4-3.

1971
Panathinaikos become the first Greek team to reach the final of the European Cup.

1981
Liverpool's Bob Paisley becomes the first manager to win the European Cup three times.

1983
Ernst Happel becomes the first and, so far, only manager to reach the European Cup or Champions League final with three different teams (Feyenoord, Club Brugge, SV Hamburg).

1984
The first penalty shootout in a European Cup final – Roma versus Liverpool.

1950s   1960s   1970s   1980s

1959
Owe Ohlsson becomes the first player to score five goals in a European Cup game during Gothenberg's 6-1 victory over Linfield.

1967
Celtic become the first British team to win the European Cup, beating Internazionale 2-1 in the final.

1969
Feyenoord beat KR Reykjavík 12–2 in the game with the most goals ever in the European Cup or Champions League.

1974
Bayern Munich become first German team to win the European Cup. They go on to win three in a row, the third club after Ajax and Real Madrid to achieve this.

1977
Gerd Müller becomes the first player to be top scorer in four European Cup seasons.

1985
The European Cup final at the Heysel Stadium, Belgium, ends in tragedy with 39 fans dying and 437 injured.

1986
Steaua Bucharest become the first team from Eastern Europe to win the European Cup.

1988
SV Werder Bremen's Manfred Burgsmüller becomes the competition's oldest scorer at the age of 38 years, 293 days, against SC Dynamo Berlin.

2000

The first Champions League or European Cup final to feature teams from the same nation, Spain, as Real Madrid defeat Valencia.

2003

Clarence Seedorf becomes the first player to win the Champions League with three different clubs (Ajax, Real Madrid and AC Milan).

1992

Barcelona win the last European Cup before the competition is relaunched as the UEFA Champions League.

2006

Arsenal's Jens Lehmann becomes the first player to be sent off in a Champions League final.

2011

Ryan Giggs becomes the only player to have scored goals in 16 different Champions League seasons.

2013

Barcelona record their sixth consecutive appearance in the Champions League semi-finals, a record.

2013

The first all-German final pits Bayern Munich against Borussia Dortmund, with Bayern claiming the trophy with a 2-1 win.

2014

Real Madrid win their tenth European Cup or Champions League title with victory over their city rivals, Atlético Madrid.

1990s　2000s　2010s

1997

UEFA expand the competition to allow second-place finishers in the top leagues of Europe to take part in the Champions League.

2007

Michael Ballack becomes the first player to reach the Champions League quarter-finals with four different clubs.

2007

Roy Makaay scores the fastest ever Champions League goal, for Bayern Munich versus Real Madrid. It is timed at just 10.12 seconds.

2009

Barcelona's Josep 'Pep' Guardiola becomes the youngest coach, at 38 years old, to win the Champions League.

2014

Cristiano Ronaldo scores the most goals in a single Champions League season, an incredible tally of 17.

2015

Bayern Munich produce an incredible quarter-final comeback from 3-1 down in the first leg versus Porto, winning 7-4 on aggregate.

2015

The Champions League final is held in Berlin's Olympiastadion. Barcelona win their fifth title by defeating Juventus 3-1, with goals from Ivan Rakitić, Luis Suárez and Neymar.

CHAMPIONS LEAGUE quiz

1. Which club won the first ever European Cup?
a) Barcelona
b) Bayern Munich
c) Real Madrid

2. In which country was the very first European Cup game played?
a) Portugal
b) England
c) France

3. Who was the youngest coach to win the competition in the Champions League era?
a) Josep Guardiola
b) Luis Enrique
c) José Mourinho

4. Which player has made more appearances in the Champions League than any other?
a) Paolo Maldini
b) Xavi Hernández
c) Philipp Lahm

5. The first Champions League group match to be played on artificial grass was staged in which country?
a) Switzerland
b) Russia
c) Cyprus

6. Who were the first champions in the Champions League era not to qualify out of the group stage the following season?
a) Internazionale
b) Porto
c) Chelsea

7. Who won the Champions League as a player with Ajax, Real Madrid and AC Milan?
a) Clarence Seedorf
b) George Weah
c) Edgar Davids

8. Who scored the Champions League's 6,000th goal?
a) Cristiano Ronaldo
b) Karim Benzema
c) Mario Götze

9. How old was Sir Alex Ferguson when he last won the Champions League with Manchester United?
a) 58
b) 66
c) 71

10. Which player became the first to top score in four European Cup or Champions League seasons?
a) Gerd Müller
b) Lionel Messi
c) Zinedine Zidane

11. Which player became the first to score in the Champions League for six different clubs?
a) David Trezeguet
b) Samuel Eto'o
c) Zlatan Ibrahimović

12. A club from which country won the European Cup for the very first time in 1986?
a) Greece
b) Romania
c) Czech Republic

13). For which club did Lars Ricken score in a Champions League final after coming onto the pitch as a substitute just 16 seconds earlier?
a) Borussia Dortmund
b) Paris Saint-Germain
c) Bayer Leverkusen

14. Which of these teams did not take part in the very first European Cup penalty shootout?
a) Ajax
b) Borussia Mönchengladbach
c) Everton

15. Who was the first coach to win the European Cup with two different clubs, the second being SV Hamburg?
a) Jupp Heynckes
b) Carlo Ancelotti
c) Ernst Happel

16. Which club became the first British side to win the European Cup?
a) Manchester United
b) Liverpool
c) Celtic

17. For which club did Philipp Lahm play seven Champions League games before appearing for Bayern Munich?
a) Stuttgart
b) Borussia Dortmund
c) SV Hamburg

18. Barcelona won their fifth Champions League title in 2015. Who did they defeat in the final?
a) Real Madrid
b) Juventus
c) Benfica

19. Against which team did Luiz Adriano score five goals in a 2014-15 Champions League game?
a) Steaua Bucharest
b) Galatasaray
c) BATE Borisov

20. Who scored the last goal of the 2014-15 Champions League season?
a) Luis Suárez
b) Neymar
c) Álvaro Morata

PICTURE CREDITS

The publishers would like to thank the following sources for their kind permission to reproduce the pictures in this book.

ALL PHOTOGRAPHY © GETTY IMAGES

T = top, B = bottom, L = left, R = right, C = centre

/Odd Andersen/AFP: 52B, 62L; /Gonzalo Arroyo Moreno: 28T; /Lars Baron/Bongarts: 60-61B, 76L; /Bongarts: 16R; /Shaun Botterill: 59T, 71BR; /Paulo Bruno: 73BL; /Clive Brunskill: 35T, 36BR; /Jean Catuffe: 72-73; /Central Press: 15BL; /Jan Christensen/FrontzoneSport: 20-21; /Fabrice Coffrini/AFP: 80; /Phil Cole: 54; /Helios de la Rubia: 3BL, 67B; /Adrian Dennis /AFP: 29B; /Epsilon: 67R; /Franck Fife/AFP: 18-19; /Christopher Furlong: 21BR; /Quique Garcia/AFP: 90; /Paul Gilham: 70; /Laurence Griffiths: 25B, 33B, 45BL, 63T, 74L; /Alex Grimm: 91; /Alex Grimm/Bongarts: 81L; /Jack Guez/AFP: 26-27T; /Valery Hache/AFP: 20BL; /Alexander Hassenstein/Bongarts: 27B, 42-43T; /Mike Hewitt: 55T, 79; /Mike Hewitt/Bongarts: 53; /Hulton Archive: 12-13; /Jasper Juinen: 86R; /Keystone-France/ Gamma-Keystone: 10-11B; /Glyn Kirk/AFP: 30-31B; /Christof Koepsel/Bongarts: 58-59, 66, 74-75; /Christopher Lee: 6-7; /Alex Livesey: 32-33T, 38-39B, 55B, 58BL, 84-85T, 85BR; /John MacDougall/AFP: 64-65; /Angel Martinez: 34-35B, 43B, 57BL, 78, 89BR; / Jamie McDonald: 56-57; /Aris Messinis/ AFP: 60BL; /Filippo Monteforte/AFP: 22-23B; /Olivier Morin/AFP: 1; /Ralph Orlowski/ Bongarts: 47B; /Valerio Pennicino: 3BR, 81BR; /Joern Pollex/Bongarts: 48-49;

/Popperfoto: 8-9, 11T, 14BL, 45R; /Anne-Christine Poujoulat/AFP: 25T, 50; /Gary M Prior: 69BR; /Professional Sport/ Popperfoto: 68L; /Ben Radford: 44-45T, 84L; /David Ramos: 73TR, 87; /Michael Regan: 76-77; /Miguel Riopa/AFP: 26; /Rolls Press/ Popperfoto: 12B; /Clive Rose: 88-89T; /Martin Rose: 31T; /Martin Rose/Bongarts: 28, 61T; /Vladimir Rys/Bongarts: 51; /Mark Sandten/ Bongarts: 52TR; /Oli Scarff/AFP: 23T; /Peter Schatz/WireImage: 68-69; /Alexandre Simoes: 56L; /Javier Soriano/AFP: 39T; /Christof Stache/AFP: 36-37T; /Patrik Stollarz/AFP: 47T; /Boris Streubel: 3BC, 37B, 62-63B, 86BL; /Sergei Supinsky/AFP: 40-41; /Bob Thomas: 14-15T, 16BL, 17; /Kenzo Tribouillard/AFP: 82-83; /VI-Images: 2; /Claudio Villa: 24-25; /Siu Wu/AFP: 46-47B.

Every effort has been made to acknowledge correctly and contact the source and/ or copyright holder of each picture and Carlton Books Limited apologises for any unintentional errors or omissions that will be corrected in future editions of this book.